GAME OF MY LIFE

DETROIT

LIONS

MEMORABLE STORIES OF LIONS FOOTBALL

PAULA PASCHE

SPORTS PUBLISHING

Sports Publishing books may be purchased in bulk at special discounts for sales promotion, corporate gifts, fund-raising, or educational purposes. Special editions can also be created to specifications. For details, contact the Special Sales Department, Sports Publishing, 307 West 36th Street, 11th Floor, New York, NY 10018 or sportspubbooks@skyhorsepublishing.com.

Sports Publishing® is a registered trademark of Skyhorse Publishing, Inc.®, a Delaware corporation.

Visit our website at www.sportspubbooks.com.

10 9 8 7 6 5 4 3 2 1

Library of Congress Cataloging-in-Publication Data is available on file.

Cover design by Tom Lau
Cover photo credit: Associated Press/Fred Jewell

ISBN: 978-1-61321-812-9
Ebook ISBN: 978-1-61321-860-0

Printed in the United States of America

For Detroit Lions fans everywhere

CONTENTS

ACKNOWLEDGEMENTS

First, much appreciation for the former and current Lions players who shared their time, reached back in the recesses of their minds and told their stories. Without them, there would be no book.

Each chapter in this book is based on a one-on-one interview with the player. All of them were conducted in person or over the phone, except in the case of Barry Sanders who responded to email questions. For the chapter on Alex Karras, who died in 2012, his son, George Karras, and teammate Charlie Sanders, shared their memories of his most memorable game. Charlie Sanders was interviewed in March 2015, four months before his death on July 2.

The game statistics were all checked using Pro Football Reference and the NFL's Game Statistics and Information Systems. Background information came from stories in the *Detroit Free Press, Detroit News,* the *Oakland Press,* the *Grand Rapids Press* and MLive.com from the clip books at the Lions facility. The quotes from players in the Calvin Johnson chapter are from the *Oakland Press* and the Associated Press. Other sources are noted.

A special thanks to all of those who helped me reach out to the players including Ryan Hackworth, the Lions community relations manager; Bill Keenist, Lions senior vice president for communications; Ben Manges, Lions director of corporate communications; Chrissie Wywrot, Risa Balayem, and Jennifer Hammond. Also thanks to Deanna Caldwell, the Lions manager of media services, for providing the photos.

Thanks to longtime Lions beat writer Mike O'Hara, who now writes for the team website, for sharing a few stories from on and off the field going way back.

I couldn't have finished this without my friends, who were always supportive even on the days that I struggled—especially Julie Jacobson Hines, Annemarie Schiavi Pedersen, and John Torchetti. Thanks from the bottom of my heart.

INTRODUCTION

While the Detroit Lions can't look back on much playoff success in recent years—their last playoff win was after the 1991 season—the history of the franchise is rich in players of talent and character.

Can't count the Super Bowl wins, because the Lions have never reached that pinnacle. But in 1935 they won their first NFL championship and followed it up in the 1950s with three more.

These days a young core of players, including Calvin Johnson and Matthew Stafford, has taken them closer to a long playoff run.

In 2014 the Lions went to the playoffs for the second time in four years. It was all good, but they aren't satisfied and won't be until they're considered a legitimate playoff contender each season.

Former Lions players know exactly what the team has gone through in the past twenty or thirty or forty years.

Al "Bubba" Baker, who played for the Lions from 1978 to 1982, said Detroit was no place to be if you hated to lose, which he did. Did he ever.

Lem Barney, who was inducted into the Pro Football Hall of Fame, played in just one playoff game in his eleven seasons with the Lions. One. Same with Hall of Famer Charlie Sanders.

Still, there are great stories from some of the best Lions players throughout the ages.

In different ways, playing for the Lions had a profound impact on their lives. That became more clear to me in every conversation, no matter the player's age, his position, or the era in which he played.

When asked to name one memorable game from their careers in Honolulu blue and silver, so many of them found a Thanksgiving game that stood out.

Back in the days before *Monday Night Football*, ESPN and the NFL Network, often the Thanksgiving games would be the only time the Lions could be seen in nationally televised games. The national spotlight seemed to bring out the best in the players whose family and friends were watching from afar.

Defensive tackle Roger Brown sacked Green Bay's Bart Starr seven times in a huge Thanksgiving win for the Lions in 1962. He and Starr have a relationship of sorts to this day. It was such a miserable experience for the Packers that coach Vince Lombardi refused to play the Lions on Thanksgiving again.

Doug English had a breakout game with four sacks in a win over the Denver Broncos on Thanksgiving in 1978.

Dre Bly's first Thanksgiving game was in 2003 when, again, the Lions made Turkey Day miserable for the Green Bay Packers. Bly intercepted Brett Favre twice that day. (Somewhere, Vince Lombardi was shaking his head.)

If you never saw Brown or English or Baker in action, you will feel like you were in the front row when you read their words.

This book is rich in history.

It contains three Hall of Famers and at least one future Hall of Famer.

You'll discover three who went into the BBQ business in retirement and another who went to culinary school in New York to become a chef.

All three men who wore the Lions' No. 20 tell their stories in these pages.

Two former players have made their mark in reality TV shows in recent years.

Most names you will recognize, a few you won't.

Lions fans are so passionate despite the disappointments over the years.

These players shared that passion for winning. Years later they remember details from their most memorable games like they were played yesterday.

Enjoy.

CHAPTER 1

BARRY SANDERS

Running back, 1989–1998

The Game: December 21, 1997 vs. the New York Jets at the Pontiac Silverdome

DETROIT LIONS 13, NEW YORK JETS 10

Barry Sanders didn't just have memorable games. All these years later, fans still remember certain plays like the time he nearly juked Tampa Bay's John Lynch out of his cleats.

He could embarrass opposing defenders, and he did quite often.

"He makes you miss so bad, you kind of look up in the stands and wonder if anybody's looking at you," Atlanta Falcons cornerback D.J. Johnson once said. "You've got 60,000 people in there and you wonder if anyone saw you miss that tackle."

Sanders, who was drafted by the Lions third overall in 1989 out of Oklahoma State, still remembers his first NFL game.

"I held out for training camp during my rookie season, so I signed three days before our opener. I remember we were playing the Phoenix Cardinals and we were down, when Coach [Wayne] Fontes put me in late in the third quarter," Sanders said.

You would think the third overall pick would get the start, but no.

"I was pretty nervous and I did not know many of the plays. They called my number on my first play in," Sanders said. "The play was designed to go to the right, but I cut back to the other side and found a hole for about 20 yards. I scored three plays later."

"I think I finished with eight carries for about 80 yards. It was pretty crazy to think I was now an NFL player," Sanders said.

In his first NFL action, he was handed the ball on four straight snaps for a total of 29 yards, ending with his first touchdown. In the official box score, which is usually comment-free, after the four lines detailing his first four carries and the touchdown, the scorekeeper wrote "The roar seemed to be restored."

Imagine that.

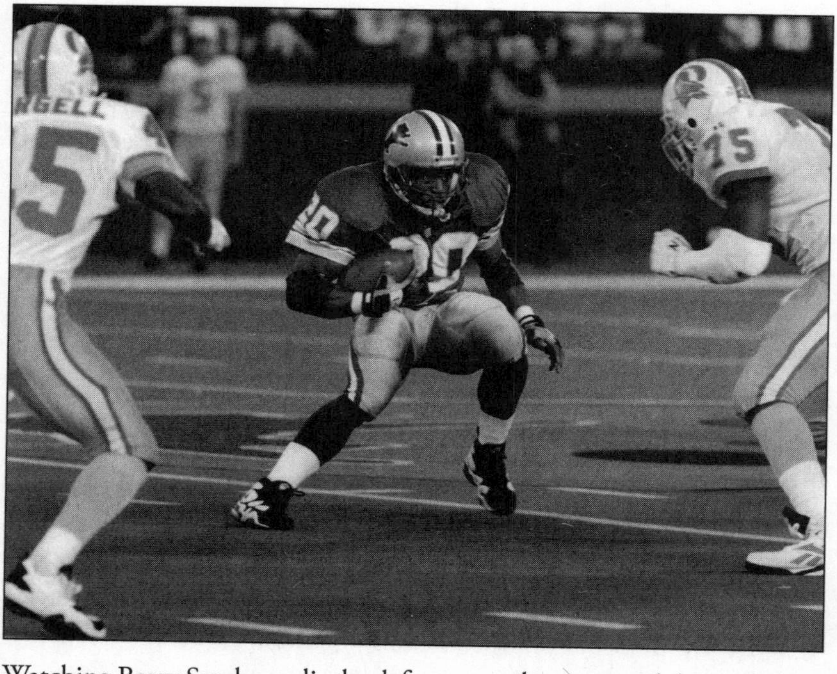

Watching Barry Sanders split the defense was always special during his ten years with the Lions. *Photo courtesy of the Detroit Lions*

That game was at the Pontiac Silverdome and gave fans and Sanders' teammates just a hint of what was to come. Since he didn't play in training camp or in preseason games, even his teammates didn't know what to expect. That included the offensive line.

In his rookie season he broke Billy Sims's single season record for yards. To thank his linemen he bought them each a Rolex watch.

That first season was the start of something magical that repeated itself over Sanders' ten seasons with the Lions. Not many players are worthy of the price of admission on their own, but Sanders was in that category. If you never had the opportunity to see him run, check out his highlights on YouTube.

Everyone in Detroit loved Barry Sanders.

"You can't ask a person in Detroit what your favorite run of Barry [is] because that would say there were just a handful and you can remember one. This guy did something special every single Sunday," long-time Pistons player and GM Joe Dumars said in the documentary *A Football Life: Barry Sanders.*

Fontes once said, "God ain't made a better back in this lifetime. Maybe one will come along someday. But it hasn't happened yet."

The Game

By Barry Sanders

"I had so many great memories of my ten years playing for the Lions, but the one moment that stands out the most was the last game of the season in 1997," Sanders said. "We were playing the Jets and needed to win to make the playoffs."

The Lions were 8–7 and the Jets 9–6. Each team needed a win for a trip to the postseason.

"I had a pretty good game and was close to getting 2,000 yards for the season. I was right around 2,000 in the fourth quarter and we were driving when I broke off a 50-plus yard run to seal the win and our playoff spot," Sanders said.

"That run also put me at 2,053 for the season. I did not really care about getting 2,000, but my linemen wanted it so badly it was extra sweet to get it for them in that fashion," Sanders said.

Everyone remembers that Sanders was never about the personal goals, but always about the wins.

It was his two-yard run in the fourth quarter that allowed him to become just the third rusher to gain 2,000 yards in a single season. The previous two were O.J. Simpson and Eric Dickerson.

On the next snap he broke for the 53-yard run that moved him into second place with 2,053 yards.

His touchdown early in the fourth quarter gave the Lions the lead for the first time that day and proved to be the game winner.

Sanders, who was named the NFL co-MVP in 1997, finished the day with 184 yards on 23 carries, for an average of eight yards per carry. It looked like he might not make it to 2,000 with just 20 yards in the first half.

But the Lions got big-time help from the defense, which intercepted the Jets quarterbacks three times.

At times that day, the Silverdome was so loud that the officials warned the Lions that it was excessive crowd noise.

But early in the fourth quarter, it was totally silent.

Linebacker Reggie Brown seriously injured his spinal cord and vertebrae making a tackle, and everyone knew it. He lay motionless on the field for seventeen minutes. Herman Moore and Johnnie Morton ran to the tunnel to roll the stretcher to the other end of the field before the ambulance made the trip out. Without quick reaction from the Lions trainer and doctors, who performed CPR, Brown might not have survived. He did survive, though his career was over; but at that moment no one knew if he would.

It was one of the games that will live forever as a memorable game for the Lions.

Obviously it's at the top of the list for Barry Sanders.

Other Memorable Moments

That 1997 season had its share of stand-out moments leading up to that final regular season game.

One of them was a win in Tampa Bay where Sanders became the only player in NFL history to score two touchdowns on runs of 80 or more yards.

To add another twist, when the Lions faced the Bucs five weeks earlier Sanders ran for 20 yards.

On October 12, 1997, in Tampa, he ran for 215 yards.

In the first quarter he scored on an 80-yard scamper and then in the third he broke free for an 82-yard touchdown run. That day he moved past Jim Brown on the all-time rushing list with 12,513 yards and also scored the game's final touchdown on a seven-yard reception. The Lions won 27–9.

The only knock against Sanders throughout his career was that, supposedly, he wasn't as effective running on grass. The Buccaneers played on a grass field.

Afterwards he told reporters he "was still learning."

Sanders' best game as a pro was on November 13, 1994, in a 14–9 win over Tampa Bay at the Silverdome.

Sanders ran for 237 yards that day, one of his four career days of more than 200 rushing yards. He had an even 200 yards in the second half.

"When Barry is hot like that, you have to give him the football," Fontes said after the game.

He outshone Bucs rookie Errict Rhett, who finished with 112 yards.

After the game, Rhett told the Associated Press, "Not only can I not do the things Barry does, I can't even describe them."

Perhaps an opposing defenseman can best describe trying to stop Sanders.

"Barry is a phenomenal running back. He's got an engine that didn't quit. A couple of missed tackles at the point of the attack, and he broke free. But that's typical Barry," Bucs defensive lineman Santana Dotson told the *Orlando Sentinel*. "To stop him, you need all eleven defensive players . . . and then you hope that a referee gets in his way."

In 1997 Sanders got off to a slow start with just 53 yards rushing combined in the first two games. Then he got serious and rushed for more than 100 yards in 14 straight games.

Of his ten seasons in Detroit, Sanders said 1991 stood out.

"The '91 season was bittersweet. It was our best season of any I had in Detroit, with a huge win over the Cowboys in the wild card game, before falling to the Redskins in the NFC Championship," Sanders said.

"That being said, we lost Mike Utley that year, so it was really a tough turn in such a great season," he added. "I love the way the team rallied for Mike and we did something special that our fans will always remember."

Mike Utley, the starting right guard, was injured on what appeared to be a routine play. But it paralyzed him from the chest down. Still, when he was strapped onto the cart to be wheeled off the field, he gave a thumbs up signal to the fans and so his teammates would know he was OK. Sanders was a regular visitor to see Utley in the hospital.

The Lions started that 1991 season with a 5–1 record, then had a hiccup after the bye week, losing three of four games to put their record at 6–4.

Utley was injured in the November 17 win over the Los Angeles Rams. The Lions finished the season with six straight wins—playing for Utley. Thumbs up was their message.

They even won the penultimate game that season at Green Bay. Through the 2014 season, the Lions had not found a way to beat the Packers in the state of Wisconsin since their 1991 victory. In that 21–17 Detroit win, Sanders had 27 carries for 85 yards.

Their 12–4 record got them into the playoffs as a wild card.

They romped over the Dallas Cowboys 38–6. Sanders had a dozen carries for 69 yards including a 47-yard touchdown scamper.

For years there was a national debate over which running back was better—Sanders or Emmitt Smith. That day Smith had more yards (15 carries, 80 yards) but it was Sanders who was on the winning side.

"It mattered that I was playing against Emmitt. He had certainly made a name for himself at that point, and I certainly wanted to put my best foot forward," Sanders said on *A Football Life.*

The Lions were confident heading to Washington the next week to play the Redskins in the NFC championship. They were one game away from going to the Super Bowl, but came up woefully short, losing to the Redskins 41–10. In that game quarterback Erik Kramer was sacked five times. The Lions were behind from the get-go, so Sanders only had 11 carries and finished with 44 yards. The Lions had lost 45–0 to the Redskins in the 1991 regular season opener.

The Aftermath

Sanders's ten years with the Lions were full of record-setting days and seasons.

He had at least 1,000 rushing yards and was elected to the Pro Bowl in each of his ten seasons. He finished his career with 15,269 rushing yards and 99 rushing touchdowns.

He also had 2,921 receiving yards and ten receiving touchdowns.

The four-time NFL leading rusher (1990, 1994, 1996, and 1997) also became the first NFL running back to record five 1,500-yard rushing seasons, in addition to being the only back to do so in four consecutive seasons (1994–1997).

Sanders was a no-brainer for the Pro Football Hall of Fame and was inducted in 2004. His father introduced him that day as the third best running back ever (behind Jim Brown and, he jokingly said, himself).

In his enshrinement speech, Barry Sanders was careful to thank all of those who had a hand in his football success.

He thanked the city of Detroit and the fans: "I had the good fortune of being drafted to a wonderful city, where people focus their life around work and business, and work and family and worship. And I fit in perfectly there because when you get drafted, you don't know where you're going to end up. And I can't think of a better place for me than Detroit. Thank you for coming out here. The fans . . . I think about my ten years there and you don't find better football fans and people who want a winner than in the city of Detroit and they supported us and come out and encouraged us to do the best we could do and I appreciate you."

Then he gave credit to Wayne Fontes who coached him his first seven seasons: "I think about my first coach, Wayne Fontes, and Wayne is a very interesting person to be around. He, Wayne, convinced me that I could become a great player and almost . . . he reminded me that if I kept on the right track and continued to be successful, that I may be as successful as he was as a player.

"In all honesty, from the first day, Coach Fontes won my admiration and he's a big reason why I'm where I am today. It was great to be around you every day coach, and I don't know where he is . . . There he is, number 20, right there. There you go. Coach Fontes was supposed to have back surgery, and I'm afraid I delayed his pain by having him come here today, but I'm grateful for his presence," Sanders added.

He didn't leave anyone out including coach Bobby Ross, his teammates, his early coaches, his hometown of Wichita and his family.

When the Lions drafted him third overall, he had been bypassed by the Cowboys, who selected Troy Aikman, and the Packers, who received heat for years for taking Tony Mandarich, who was a bust.

Sanders had won the Heisman Trophy at Oklahoma State in 1988.

Like Billy Sims, he didn't start out playing running back in high school. He played cornerback and wingback until his senior year. When the regular tailback was suspended for disciplinary reasons, Sanders took his spot and gained a school-record 274 yards and four touchdowns.

At Oklahoma State he set or tied 24 NCAA records. In his three seasons with the Cowboys he accumulated 3,797 yards and 55 touchdowns.

Like Calvin Johnson, Sanders has always been humble.

Apart from his amazing moves, he wasn't flashy, didn't do touchdown dances. He scored 109 TDs in his Lions career (ten receiving). Afterward, he would always hand the football to the official—you know, like he'd been there before.

Chapter 2

CALVIN JOHNSON

Wide receiver, 2007–present

The Game: December 22, 2012 vs. the Atlanta Falcons at Ford Field

ATLANTA FALCONS 31, DETROIT LIONS 18

Calvin Johnson is a man of few words.

It's just his way.

As mind-blowing as some of his catches are, the Lions wide receiver remains humble.

He doesn't seek the spotlight; it just seems to find him.

Maybe it has something to do with the highlight reel catches that are just the norm for the man known as Megatron.

His teammates will gladly heap on the accolades.

On October 27, 2013, Johnson had 329 receiving yards on 14 of 16 receiving in a 31–30 comeback win over the Dallas Cowboys at Ford Field. It was the second-most receiving yards in a single game in NFL history.

"I'd have to say that win against the Cowboys, that was a crazy game in my career," Johnson said.

It wasn't a shocker really.

This is what he does.

His teammates have seen it all in games and even at practice where Johnson does not hold back.

Here's what some of the Lions had to say to the media that day:

- "I've literally never seen anything like that before in my life. He's the greatest receiver in the history of the National Football League."—Lions running back Reggie Bush.
- "I have not ever seen anything like that. As a receiver, you're like, yeah, 100 yards would be a great day. I can't tell you what 300 would do. That's probably more receiving yards than I've got on the season. So that tells you something right there."—Lions wide receiver Kris Durham.
- "Amazing. Nothing more you have to say about him. . . . It shouldn't surprise me, but it just amazes me every time. I mean, you should hear it out there. We're in the pocket and it's, 'Oh, my God! Oh, my God!' It's crazy."—Lions veteran center Dominic Raiola.
- "The greatest."—left guard Rob Sims.
- "That's some Madden stuff right there."—rookie right guard Larry Warford.
- "Going up and catching that ball on the first play, Calvin Johnson on a safety is as good of a match-up you're going to get. The guy goes up and makes a freak-show catch. He does it all the time." "The best thing about that dude is how humble he is and how much of a team player he is. I can't express it enough to you guys. I say it, but you guys don't really know it because you're not in the locker room with him. But he's a heck of a teammate and everybody respects the heck out of him. He's a self-less player, a guy that works his tail off to sometimes get ready to play. He catches the ball however many times today and gets hit all the time. . . . He made some big-time catches at some big-time moments."—Lions quarterback Matthew Stafford.

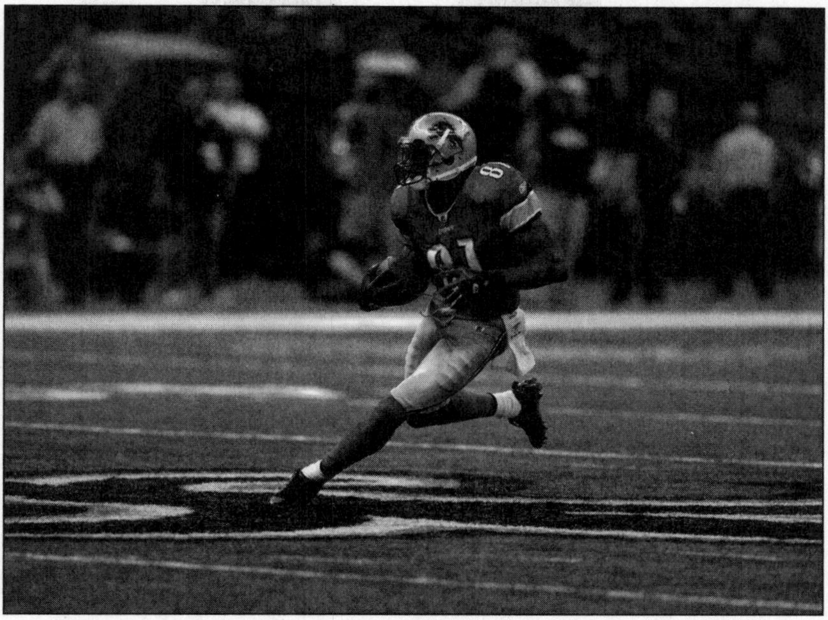

Calvin Johnson finds space on the field on a routine basis. *Photo courtesy of the Detroit Lions*

- "Just wait until he's 100 percent."—Coach Jim Schwartz referring to fact Johnson was coming off a leg injury.

As expected, Johnson didn't have too much to say about his unbelievable day.

"It's crazy you know, shoot, we got one-on-one coverage," Johnson told reporters. "I don't know what our percentages were we were able to hit on a lot of deep passes, intermediate, we were all over the place."

The Lions finished with 623 yards of offense—356 more than the Cowboys.

It was quite the game.

And yet that game against the Cowboys is not Calvin Johnson's most memorable game. It is a standout and he mentioned it as a contender, but the game that stands out for him was when he broke

Jerry Rice's record for receiving yards in a single season, which had stood since 1995 at 1,848.

It was a special season for Johnson, no doubt about it.

That day was almost perfect.

The Game

By Calvin Johnson

"I broke the record; that was a big-time game. It's not easy to decide since there were so many big games," Johnson said. "It's definitely that one."

Johnson needed 182 yards that day to break Rice's record. It certainly wasn't a lock.

But he said there was no added pressure. He still had another game in the season to break the record.

"I just kind of went with it," Johnson said. 'When it's game time the job's in front of you, when you have the opportunity to take advantage, you just do it."

His second reception that day was for 49 yards on a pass from Matthew Stafford.

All of a sudden, it looked like it might be easy.

"Coming off the first reception, right off the bat early in the game, I went to the sideline I don't know who I was talking to, my coach he might have said we don't [have to worry] today."

Johnson said that in some games, it's apparent early that everything will fall his way.

"It doesn't happen as much as you want it to; [but] there are games where you can tell early," Johnson said.

When he made the record breaking catch—his tenth of the game—it was on a first-and-10 from the Lions' 20-yard line. It was the same route he'd run earlier in the game without success. He knew that was the moment. It put him over 200 yards for the day, but more importantly, it put him ahead of Rice in the record book.

The crowd at Ford Field erupted, because the fans knew, too.

Johnson took the ball to the sideline and handed it to his father who was waiting.

That is the precise moment that made the day.

"There were a lot of games, but that was special because my dad was there," said Johnson, an only child who is close with his family.

"It was I think a big symbol of the hard work that I've seen him put in, translate that onto the field and all the hard work I've put in in my profession," Johnson said. "There's a lot of correlations I could come up with."

Even with his son earning one of the richest NFL contracts ever, his dad had kept his job with the railroad in Atlanta. He and Calvin's mom, who works for a school system, set the example for their son for hard work.

They got to celebrate the results that day.

Offhand, Johnson couldn't even recall if the Lions had won that game. It was the seventh straight loss in a disappointing season for the Lions, who had made the playoffs in 2011.

Johnson's road to the record added a sweet moment to an otherwise sour season.

Not surprisingly, Johnson gave credit to Stafford.

"It's half his, too, you know, he's the one delivering me the ball every week," Johnson said that day. "When we both stay healthy man we can do some special things out there."

Johnson addressed his teammates after the game.

"You know Calvin, he didn't say a whole lot," Stafford told reporters. "But he told us he appreciated our hard work and our help to get him there and he thought it was a team thing—exactly what you would think Calvin Johnson would say is what he said and I'm just proud to be associated with him."

After the game, coach Jim Schwartz told reporters: "I've been an NFL fan my whole life, dating back to watching Johnny Unitas and Raymond Berry as a kid, and I've coached in this league for nineteen years. I've seen a lot of Hall of Famers, but I've never seen a better player than Calvin Johnson. He just broke a record set by Jerry Rice, who is arguably the best player in the history of this league."

Hard to top that memory.

Other Memorable Moments

Johnson finished that game with 1,892 yards. The next week, the final game of the 2012 season, he would add 72 more. So the record now stands at 1,964. Of any wide receiver who has a chance to break it, Johnson might have the best odds.

Breaking Rice's record was just one of the milestones hit by Johnson in that loss to the Falcons.

On the same record-breaking 26-yard catch, he also set an NFL record for his fourth straight 10-catch game.

When he went over the 100-yard mark earlier that game he set an NFL record with eight consecutive games of 100-plus yards. He also tied Michael Irvin for the NFL record of 11 100-yard receiving games in a season.

Johnson set a Lions franchise record for most receiving yards in a season on his second catch of the night—a 49-yard pass play from quarterback Matthew Stafford. He surpassed Herman Moore, who set the record of 1,686 yards in 1995.

So let's just get this over with now.

Johnson's name is all over the NFL and the Lions' record books:

- Two-time NFL receiving yards leader for a season in 2011 and 2012
- NFC receiving touchdowns leader in 2010 and 2011
- Second most all-time receiving yards in a game with 329

- Only player in NFL history with 5,000-plus receiving yards in a three-year period
- Pro football record for most career games with 200-plus receiving yards five times, which ties him with Lance Alworth
- Lions all-time leader in receiving yards and touchdowns
- Fastest receiver to reach 10,000 receiving yards in the NFL

Also:

- Selected for the Pro Bowl five times (2010–2014)
- Three-time first team All-Pro (2011, 2012, 2013)
- Ranked No. 2 in the Top 100 Players of 2014
- Ranked No. 3 in the Top 100 players of 2013
- Ranked No. 3 in the Top 100 players of 2012
- Ranked No. 27 in the Top 100 players of 2011

Herman Moore still owns the Lions records for most receptions in a career with 670. Johnson needs 28 to take over in that category.

Moore also owns the franchise record for most receptions in a season with 123 (1995). Johnson had 122 in 2012.

He also has a dubious honor. There's an NFL rule on completing a catch that has been named the Calvin Johnson rule.

Johnson made what appeared to be a game-winning touchdown catch at Chicago in the first game of the 2010 season. However, it was overturned because players who fall to the ground while catching a pass must maintain control of the ball "throughout the process of contacting the ground."

"The process"—those are the key words.

The NFL has discussed changing the rule but has so far stood with it. Johnson was victim of it again in the Lions' 2013 opener against the Vikings. On a 20-yard touchdown pass, Johnson got two feet down and appeared to control the ball as it broke the plane of the goal line. Upon further review, it was determined that he didn't maintain control all the way, and the catch was ruled incomplete.

Even Johnson was confused that day about the rule. "Yeah, they got me again," he told reporters. "I'm going to have about four different pictures in there (the rulebook). I caught the ball, and my feet touched, and then I dove in. I mean, I don't know."

So he marches on.

After reading his list of accomplishments, it's hard to imagine that fans were second-guessing Lions' management in 2007. Johnson didn't have a rip-roaring rookie season and fans were up in arms (imagine that) because they weren't sure he was worth the second overall pick.

After all, they could have had Adrian Peterson or Joe Thomas or Patrick Willis.

Johnson missed a few days of training camp as a rookie while contract negotiations continued. He agreed on a whopping six-

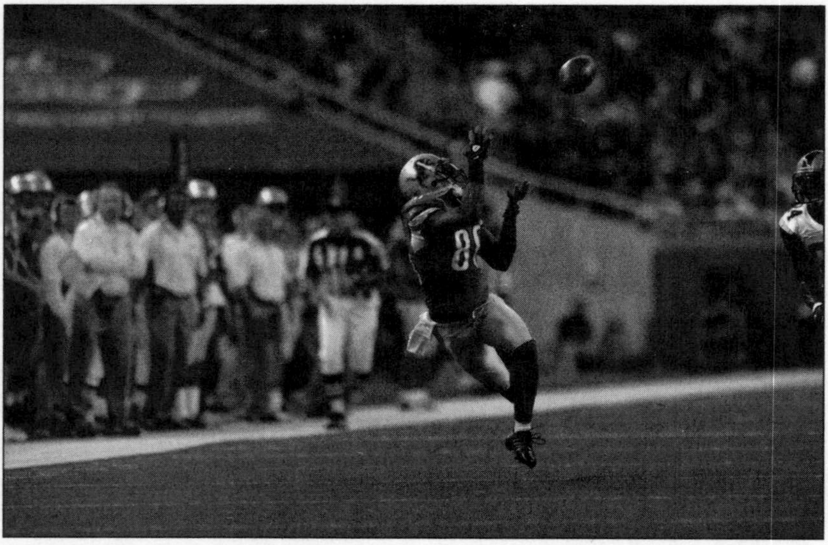

Matthew Stafford knows he just has to get the ball in the vicinity of Calvin Johnson and he'll do the rest. *Photo courtesy of the Detroit Lions*

year, $55.5 million contract that includes almost $27.2 million in guarantees. With bonuses, the contract has a maximum value of $64 million, and it makes him the highest-paid player in Lions history.

Even though he had won the Biletnikoff Award as the best receiver in college and even though many experts considered him the best player in the 2007 draft (the Raiders took quarterback JaMarcus Russell with the first overall pick), his teammates weren't sure what to expect from him in his first game.

That included quarterback Jon Kitna, who was riding the fence.

"He's still a rookie. If you're looking for him to just explode and average 100 yards every week early on in the season, I don't think that's going to be the case. . . . " Kitna told MLive.com. "But the speed of the game changes from [off-season practices] to training camp to now, going to opening day. The speed of the game changes, and those are things you have to adjust to. The other guys, they've seen it, and they know it, and they know what to expect. But then again, he is pretty dominant."

He wasn't done.

"And he will be working against somebody that definitely isn't as tall as him, and he runs as fast as them, so he's going to have a chance to make some big plays for us every week, and, certainly, this week is no different," Kitna said.

Johnson remembers his first game as a rookie well. It was a big 36–21 road win for the Lions.

"It was cool because you started out in Oakland, you could sense you're in a special kind of stadium," Johnson said. "To go out and actually win the first game and score a touchdown, it was cool."

In that game he grabbed his first NFL touchdown on a 16-yard pass from Jon Kitna in the third quarter. It put the Lions up 17–0. Johnson had four catches for 70 yards in his first game.

He scored another touchdown in his second game, but in the third game of his rookie season, he fell and acquired a deep bone bruise in his lower back. He went on to play most of the rest of the season, but he was never really the same. Hence the outcry from the fans.

Johnson stayed away from the media as much as possible in his rookie season. He knew they would ask about his back and he did not want to talk about it.

And he didn't until the spring of 2008 when he talked to MLive.com: "I was on meds the rest of the season. I was taking Vicodin twice a game just to get through the game," Johnson said. "I stayed hurt the whole season, probably because I was trying to come back too soon. But I'm not going to be the kind of guy who's going to say 'I can't do this or this because I'm hurt.' I'm not going to say that.

"I've played with injuries before, but I've never had anything like this," Johnson said.

He nearly doubled his yardage from his rookie season (756) in his second year in 2008 when he finished with 1,331. Mind you that was the season the Lions went 0–16.

In his third season, 2009, he fell just short of 1,000 receiving yards (984) but hasn't fallen below 1,000 since then. In his second and third seasons, the Lions managed to win just two of 32 games.

It seems fans no longer wonder if Matt Millen, the general manager at the time, made the right decision with Johnson.

The Aftermath

One thing has stuck with Johnson all these years. It's the nickname "Megatron" that was given to him by former teammate Roy Williams. The name comes from a Transformers character who is actually a bad guy, the nemesis of Optimus Prime.

Johnson is no bad guy, but Megatron is a name that has stuck.

It's not just in Detroit; his catches have made him popular around the NFL.

In April 2012, he was announced as the winner of the contest to be on the cover of the Madden NFL '13 video game. In the end it came down to Megatron vs. Panthers quarterback Cam Newton with Johnson winning 52 percent of the 651,000 votes in the final stage of the competition. He, of course, said he was "shocked."

"Man, it's great," a smiling Johnson said during the announcement in New York. "Just to see yourself on this Madden [cover] and seeing all the guys that have been on Madden? C'mon, man."

That award came after the 2011 season, the one season in the first eight seasons that was a real standout for Johnson.

The Lions started 5–0.

"When we went to the playoffs in New Orleans, that was a memorable season," Johnson said. "We got off to a good start. A lot of the guys we had on the team at the time, I still keep in contact with them, not that I don't with the other teams. But a lot of good guys we had on the team and helped us get as far as we did."

A good start? Yes, and Johnson played a huge role.

He caught eight touchdown passes in the first four games, all wins.

Still, former NFL receiver Cris Carter was not impressed. During a radio appearance ahead of the 2011 season, Carter didn't include Johnson in his list of top five NFL receivers.

Possibly Johnson's biggest fan, his teammate Nate Burleson, sat a few lockers away. While Johnson said he wasn't bothered by Carter's comments, Burleson took offense.

"I feel like right now Calvin Johnson is definitely in the top five and arguably the best receiver in the game—at his height, his strength, his ability to jump there, aren't too many receivers that can do what he does, period," Burleson said. "His speed is incredible, he jumps a 45-inch vertical, he has huge hands, he can bench press 225, as much as linebackers."

Responding to Carter's comment that "you don't have to double-team [Johnson] to take him out of the game," Burleson said he'd love for opposing defensive coordinators to take that advice. "If you single cover Calvin Johnson, I guarantee we'll win nine times out of ten," Burleson said.

In that 2011 season, Stafford led the offense to three fourth-quarter comebacks.

None was more spectacular than the 28–27 win at the Oakland Raiders on December 18 that year. The Lions were down by two touchdowns in the fourth quarter and came back to win.

"It was another one of those games where you have to know you're going to get fed the whole game, there's going to be plenty of opportunities on the table that's my attitude just take advantage of the opportunities you're going to get," Johnson said. "That was another one that coach told me from the beginning of the game they were going to feed me because of the coverage we were getting that day."

Johnson had nine catches for 214 yards and a pair of touchdowns in that win. Stafford, who calls it his most memorable game, threw for 391 yards, four touchdowns, and no interceptions. The Lions needed that win to keep their hopes alive for the playoffs.

The long plane ride home rates as one of the best trips back from the West Coast.

"We won the game with great passes, we had to come from a deficit in the fourth quarter," Johnson said. "It was amazing. It's a long ride, nobody slept, everybody was up talking, that was a good ride."

The Lions won the next game to clinch a playoff spot, a wildcard game against New Orleans, the first playoff game for Johnson in his first five seasons.

"It was a lot of excitement you had to almost turn down your emotions because it was such a big game," said Johnson. Unfortunately, the Lions went on to lose to the Saints, 45–28.

As painful as the loss was, it did help him and the rest of the offense know what to expect when they returned to the playoffs in 2014.

Johnson is careful to give credit to his teammates and, in particular, to quarterback Matthew Stafford. The two have been together since Stafford was drafted with the first overall pick in 2009.

Stafford has the arm strength and knows he just has to get the ball in the vicinity of Johnson.

The Lions have built the offense around the talent of those two, and they have developed quite the bond in their years together.

One great example comes from that 2011 season in a game at Dallas when the Lions were down 27–3 in the third quarter. The Lions' defense returned two interceptions for touchdowns to get Detroit back in the contest.

Then Stafford and Johnson connected for a pair of touchdowns. On the first one, from 23 yards out, Stafford passed to Johnson in the end zone.

"That's a play where I'll give a lot of credit to coach [Scott] Linehan," Stafford said after the game. "He drew it up early in the week and knew that if we get in this situation they're going to protect the first shot to Calvin and it obviously didn't move to where we thought they might move on defense. Calvin just kind of looked at me and told me to throw it up. That's a good enough sign for me. He had good position on him. I threw a ball up there and he went and got it. It's just what he does."

Johnson actually caught Stafford's eye and pointed his finger toward the heavens.

"It's a designed play. If we get the favorable coverage, it could come to me, but obviously we didn't, but at the same time, Matt saw me and I saw him, we made contact, and I just put my finger up for him to put it up for me," Johnson said after the game.

That is why the two are so successful. They respect each other and have good communication on and off the field.

Away from football, Johnson is just as good of a guy as he is on it. Of course it has something to do with his parents and the way he was raised. He displayed this while in college at Georgia Tech where he majored in building construction.

He was given a choice one summer of helping out with designs for environmentally friendly luxury condos near the campus or going to Bolivia to design and build solar latrines to improve sanitation. Of course he went to Bolivia because he wanted to help the less fortunate.

Since he's arrived in the NFL he created the Calvin Johnson Jr. Foundation whose motto is "catching dreams." His mother, Dr. Arica Johnson, is the vice president and co-executive director.

The foundation awards college scholarships to deserving student athletes in Atlanta and Detroit.

Although it's much more than that. It has fed countless needy families in Detroit and Atlanta and in 2012 it provided scholarships and sponsorship to ten impoverished children of Haiti.

Johnson's not going anywhere soon.

Even though he played with injuries through most of the 2014 season, the Lions do not think he is fading into the sunset.

In March 2012, Johnson signed an eight-year, $150.5 million deal that keeps him under contract in Detroit through 2019.

The coaching staff led by Jim Caldwell and offensive coordinator Joe Lombardi pinch themselves when they realize what kind of wide receiver they have on their roster.

Early into offseason workouts in 2014, Lombardi assessed Johnson this way: "You have to be careful not to be a fan when you're watching him. It's really unbelievable when you see him in person just how big and strong and fast he is. It's even more so than you thought. It's impressive."

CHAPTER 3

AL "BUBBA" BAKER

Defensive end, 1978–1982

The Game: October 22, 1978 vs. the San Diego Chargers at the Pontiac Silverdome

DETROIT LIONS 31, SAN DIEGO CHARGERS 14

To whom much is given, much is expected. That fits Al "Bubba" Baker's five seasons with the Detroit Lions. At least partly.

Baker was paid $25,000 in his rookie season as a second-round draft pick. He didn't make much more in the following seasons. He had to work an extra job in the offseason, every offseason.

However much was expected from the 6-foot-6, 250-pound defensive end.

Defensive coordinator Floyd Peters made sure of that. And, at the time, Baker hated him for it.

"I was twenty years old, when you're twenty you think that everybody should be treated equally. But realistically as I grew as a man and got my own kids, you can't treat people the same," Baker said. "You can have the same rules, but going back to those redeeming qualities, he thought that I had more ability so he expected more of me. That doesn't bode well when you're in your twenties.

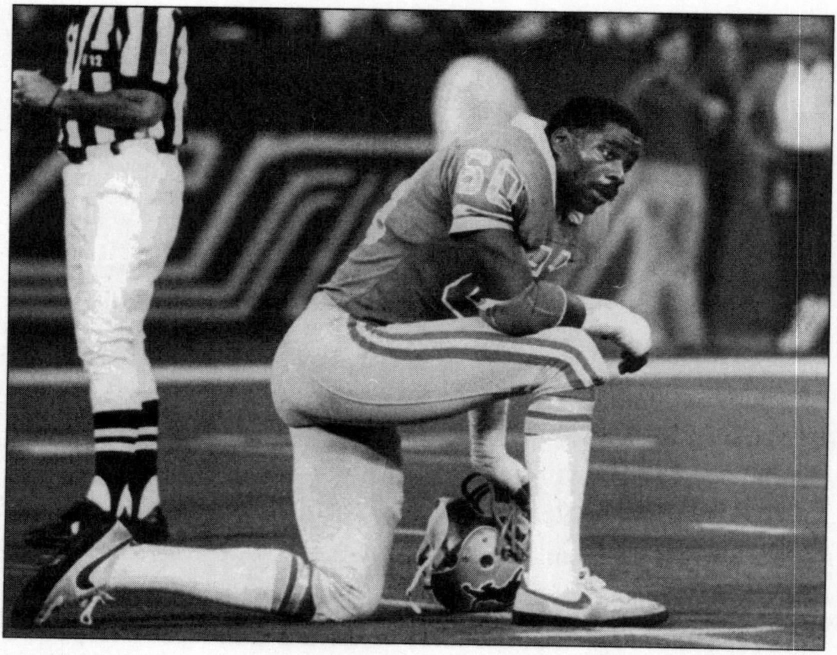

Al "Bubba" Baker notched 23 sacks as a rookie in 1978. *Photo courtesy of the Detroit Lions*

"When you're twenty years old, you're just trying to do just enough to stay good. But for Floyd for me, good was the enemy of great. I didn't see that then, that's why I detested this man—the smell of his cologne, his cigarettes, his coffee, everything.

"I absolutely [was] appalled [by] this man, I wanted to kill him seriously. Then we have this professional relationship. He made me successful, you get what I'm saying," Baker said.

As an older, wiser man Baker concedes that Floyd Peters made him who he was.

In his thirteen-year NFL career, Baker went to the Pro Bowl three times. Heck, thanks to Peters, he was NFL defensive rookie of the year in 1978 with 23 sacks.

For Baker, it all goes back to one game in his rookie season. It wasn't so much the result of the game—although the Lions won—it was the unique style of preparation by Floyd Peters.

"Let's just put it this way, the story is as much about Floyd and us. As a group we were called the Silver Rush," said Baker who played on the unit with Doug English, Dave Pureifory, and Hall of Famer Curley Culp.

The Game

By Bubba Baker

So this particular week we were getting ready to play Dan Fouts' San Diego Chargers.

On Mondays we would run and he would coach us. We'd get lined up in our positions and we'd walk through. And typically it would start with him, he'd start with Pureifory and say "You're a man's man, you played well and had two hits on the quarterback," and he'd coach off the previous game. He'd go to the next guy. Then he'd go to Doug English and say, "Doug, you did what you always do blah, blah, blah."

He'd get to me and say, "Do you think you played your best game? I know you had two sacks and you had seven tackles, but I saw quite a few plays where I thought you could've made better plays."

That was his way of constantly applying pressure to me and so that was normal. No matter how high I performed he coached me. He never allowed me personally to feel like I did good, that I did my best and he thought I could have done better. He was right 99.9 percent of the time. You hate when somebody else is in your head.

Now on the Monday before the Chargers' game, Floyd Peters walks over and he says to Pureifory, "You know Dave, I don't expect you to be able to get around the corner because this guy takes three steps, he's just going to push you by." Then he walks off.

Then he goes over to Curley Culp and he says, "Curley, as strong as you are, they got three guys—they're just not going to let you get any middle pressure." He goes on and on, then he goes down to Doug.

"Doug, you just give me what you got. I don't expect you guys to be able to beat these guys, you just played last week." He'd never done this ever—he'd always coached us up.

He gets down to me and says, "I know you're used to having your way with guys, this guy here, more than likely you won't smell the quarterback. These guys do a great job of keeping Fouts clean." Then he walks off.

That whole week that was the coaching. He would show us the film, "Look at how none of these guys are not getting anywhere near Fouts, he's got all day long to throw." He just continued down this path.

That was the one week I was actually planning to kill him. I had about six other guys who were going to help me—we were going to run him over with a car or something, poison him. We were trying to find out how we were going to kill this man this week. Seriously, we were that close to planning his demise.

There's a day called offensive day and a day called defensive day. On defensive day you go over what your plan of attack will be against these folks. He walks off, I'll never forget it like it was yesterday. He said something to the effect, "You guys just give it your best and fight like men." He was implying that we were not going to be able to get to Fouts.

In the game we sacked Fouts eleven times and I had five sacks.

I didn't talk to Floyd for a long time after that. He never did it again. The following week he went back to being a horse's ass and doing what he does. We had to run three gassers (on Monday), he went back to treating us like he usually did. He only did that in the four years he coached me one time—that week.

He got the results that he wanted. That was for us to take it out on Dan Fouts. When I see Fouts now, he still talks about that day. But it was the most brilliant strategy pulled at the perfect time. He literally was saying to us, "You guys can't beat these guys."

He did not coach us that week, he did not coach us. "Just give me your best, fight like men." We were cursing him, saying, "What the hell was going on?"

I remember riding back from Monday's practice with Pureifory. We never said a word to each other. It took us about a day to understand what was happening. We had that Tuesday off and nobody talked to each other. We came back on Wednesday, we were kind of like "What the hell was that on Monday?" And so he followed it up on Wednesday.

I think I looked at more film that week than the rest of my career added up. To me the brilliance of it was that he picked that week, he picked that team, he picked that particular means of getting us to a level of wanting to make him out to be wrong.

They were called something like Air Coryell (named for Chargers coach Don Coryell). They were flying high (they were 6.5-point favorites on the road) and it was true, nobody was getting to Fouts.

However many sacks it was, it was national news because we ripped them to shreds. He couldn't throw; he couldn't even breathe. If it wasn't me hitting him, it was another guy. We weren't hitting him all at the same time, we just hit often.

We were playing like men on fire and it had to do with this brilliant—now I'm twenty, twenty-one, twenty-two years old I don't even realize what's being done to me. I just know I hate Floyd. The rest of us felt pretty much the same about him.

He caused us to be respected throughout the National Football League and he coached us apart from the rest of the team.

You could almost say that coach Monte Clark felt like "Floyd, handle your boys," that was kind of how he was. Everybody knew it, we were like we were sort of like Floyd's Goons. We were like the Marines.

In fact, he had a saying whenever one of us—pretty much most of the time it was me—who was too close to quarterback Gary Danielson in practice. Back then, that's when it started, you're not supposed to get near his arm, he could hit your helmet. I would always push him and hit him, I would actually. I was working on my game. I had my strategy I wanted to get a good lathering that week so I wasn't really, it was hard for me to see that whole thing.

Gary Danielson had on a red jersey and we weren't supposed to actually touch him. I touched him as much as possible. That annoyed the hell out of Monte. That was part of my job, that's what they drafted me for, they didn't know that. I drove Monte Clark crazy by interrupting his practices, by doing what I did best and that was rush the passer.

This was the game that stood out as a Detroit Lion the most because our coach, who threw us under the bus and said, "I don't expect you guys to be the Silver Rush" and later find out that was the intended strategy—to tick us off to the point where we took it out on Fouts.

I was hoping he would continue to be that person. The following Monday he went back to being the horse's ass that he always was. To me it was the most brilliant coaching strategy ever employed on me in my thirteen-year career. I have never seen that or ever seen it again from any other coach. In fact, he wouldn't even discuss it. Some ten years later when I went to play for him in Minnesota, he acted like he had no idea what I was talking about. He took no credit for it.

Other Memorable Moments

"I played for Floyd '78, '79, '80, and then my fourth year was '81 he left and then I did not see him again until '88 in Minnesota. He still rode me and I was in my eleventh year, still did the same thing that I had this magic thing inside me and I hadn't tapped it yet. I understood by then what he was doing," Baker said.

"I would leave Mondays thinking to myself how can I box this guy in his head? Again, my rookie year I had 23 sacks because of him. I had 16, then 18. I never, ever played at that level again until '88. He was that guy, that's why that game stands out to me more than any other game.

"Not so much as my own individual play, the fact that was probably the last man that's ever been in my head," Baker said. "That actually got into my head and actually got a positive result from being in my head.

"We don't like people pointing out our mistakes, none of us like that. My wife and I will start having a conversation, I'll immediately stop her and say, 'Will you do me a favor? Don't think for me, please don't say what's on my mind.'

"'I know what's on your mind, Al,' she says.

"By the way that guy left an impression on me. I literally took the principles I learned from him the good side of it, because he always had our backs. If Monte or somebody else would say, 'Floyd what are we going to do about Baker jumping offsides?' Floyd would say, 'Hey Monte it's part of it, he's a hair-trigger for us.' 'What can we do to get him to back up off the ball?' and Floyd would say, 'No, I want him to cheat up on the ball as close as he can and if they don't catch it we're good.'"

Baker kept in touch with Peters through the years.

"He passed away about four Christmases ago. He had dementia and he passed away," Baker said. "He's in pass-rush heaven.

"Right before he went away, actually one Christmas we talked. He was a little sketchy—I said, 'Coach do you know what you're talking about? He would always say—this is well after my career—he would say, 'You know you were always the most talented guy I had.' He never would say he'd ride my rear end. I saw more in you . . . I was like 'Floyd, that's crap. You rode my ass.'

"He was like a father figure, a drill instructor figure. If it were not for Floyd Peters my name would not be coming up in Hall of Fame ballots, it was purely because of him and the guys I played with that had the unique qualities that he brought out," Baker said. "He did that with every guy that was there. He'd find out what that quality was. He'd say 'Bill Gay, this is all I want you to do and I expect you to not only do it but I expect you to do it at a very high level.' Whatever that quality was if you did not perform at that level, you had a real bad day when you met with Floyd," Baker said.

"The guys today, the players today, could not have played for this man. More mentally tough, I mean you know we had moves, you had to run on Monday—this is one of my favorite things in my story," Baker said. "No matter what we did on Sunday, you had to run three gassers on Monday. You had to run it in thirty-eight seconds that's across the field the short way—across back, across back and across back and run through the line. Every Monday, he believed that no matter how sore you were if you ran you got this lactic acid out of you."

On Mondays these days in the NFL, players sometimes meet and might have a walk-through looking at their mistakes from Sunday. They might get massages, but they do not run gassers.

"One other thing I left out, guys couldn't play for him today. I went through most of my life because as a young man because this is what Floyd would say: 'Baker, you are the only black guy that I ever coached that didn't get that extra muscle.' Meaning I wasn't fast. Bill Gay could run, Bill Gay was a very good athlete, he was the best athlete of us all, that was his redeeming quality. He was a tight end that came over to play defense because he couldn't catch. So Floyd would say, 'Look at Bill go. Hell of a play. Bill, he's got that extra muscle.' Two plays later I'd do something, he'd go, 'Now Baker you never got that extra muscle.'

"So I go through life thinking black people have an extra muscle in their leg because that's what Floyd Peters said. You talk to any of us guys he would say that. . . . Here I am I'm All-Pro.

"I think he felt like he had to keep me in line, keep me from going over the edge because I lived on the edge. When I say to you that people today couldn't play for him, today he'd be on CNN or ESPN: 'The guy's a racist. He's saying that black people got the extra muscle.'"

Safe to assume, Floyd Peters was in Baker's head back then and maybe a little still now from up above in pass-rush heaven.

"He never let anybody else coach us during the game; we were his guys," Baker said. "We were a special band, the Silver Rush was held to the highest esteem. We were respected by the rest of the team. I've never had any other relationship—for the rest of my career I searched for that.

"Why are we faster, bigger, stronger and we can't play together like we did in Detroit? It was Floyd.

"The hardest lesson I learned was it was who was in charge that made us click like we did," Baker said.

As much as Baker learned to respect Peters, he didn't see eye to eye with head coach Monte Clark.

"Of course I said something in the media like I always needed to do, Monte wasn't real happy with me," Baker said. "I was an All-Pro, I'm in my second or third year, hey I'm a part of this team. . . .

"I'm thinking his beef was me. I didn't have any fear as a kid, if I could take it back I would. I honestly said what was on my mind. We all know in hindsight that doesn't make you the smartest guy in the room. . . .

"When you're twenty-three or twenty-four you think that telling people what's really on your mind will get you what you want. Obviously later in life, I got married and I realized it takes a bigger man to shut up than to have the last word," Baker said.

Baker spent five years (1978–1982) with the Lions and also played for the St. Louis Cardinals (1983–1986), the Cleveland Browns (1987 and 1989–1990), and the Minnesota Vikings (1988).

"I later found out, I never knew this until I got to Cleveland that I was a sore loser," Baker said. "Honestly, I didn't lose well . . . It hit me when we lost, I realized that losing didn't sit well with me and that we lost so much in Detroit what Monte was trying to get me to do was be a pleasant loser and I wasn't I was a sore loser. To this day, I still am, to this day."

It's just that he has learned to pick his moments.

"I internalize it now, I have a forty-eight-hour rule and I wait to talk to staff or family member. Some people have a twenty-four-hour rule. I have a forty-eight-hour rule because when I was younger I hurt myself, not intentionally I didn't know what I was doing. I thought my opinion counted and it didn't."

In the five seasons Baker played for the Lions they had an accumulated record of 30–43 (1982 was a strike year).

"The Detroit Lions back then, we were notorious for finding a way to lose. If there was a way to lose, we did it. Probably the most frustrating year was the year when David Hill, Jimmy Allen, and James Hunter made that song 'Another One Bites the Dust.' We were 6–0 and did not make the playoffs. That's how I remembered us, if there was a way we could screw up we found it and we did it.

"For me it was very, very frustrating to have two games to go and you're playing for nothing . . . That was a real tough sell for me. . . . In hindsight as I look back at it, I was very ashamed when we lost because we were playing good enough to win on defense but we had some challenges on offense," Baker said.

"It was a completely different team at home with our fans than when we were on the road. I thought it was because we didn't have a bully mentality, we had a passive mentality—we wanted to outsmart you, out trick you," Baker said.

"You weren't supposed to comment on those things and I did like a big dope," Baker said. "You look back at when you were younger and think, 'Wow I wish I would have handled that different.'

"I thought I was respected," Baker said. "More than anything I loved breaking that guy in front of me's will. I loved kicking his butt. I lived for it. I thought the whole game should be played.

"You get the right to be stupid and dumb as a young kid, that was me, that was my role," Baker said. "To this day it hurts me from going into the Hall of Fame, that's a close-knit group of guys and a lot of my accomplishments have been over-shadowed because I marched to the beat of a different drum."

The sad thing—that Baker still thinks about—is that he didn't find a way to enjoy his NFL playing days.

"Now I understand God and I can laugh about things. Anything that I'm remiss in is that I didn't enjoy playing when I was playing. You couldn't enjoy it because of the pressure to play at a high standard. There were only fifty-six defensive ends in the world, and what drove me was I didn't want to lose my job," Baker said.

"I applied pressure to myself twenty-four hours a day, seven days a week. How are you going to enjoy that? Now I'm one of millions of guys who make barbecue and I still make a living. The only way I could make a living that way is I had to be on one of those twenty-eight football teams or I was a failure.

"As a result there was not fun in that, there was the accolades that came with being famous, but back then $25,000 a year wasn't a fortune. You didn't have fame and fortune, you had fame. Everybody knew me, but we didn't make no money. I had a job my whole thirteen years in the offseason that I had to work. My rookie contract was for $25,000.

"After defensive lineman of the year and NFL rookie of the year, I wanted a new contract but you know the Lions that wasn't going to happen. So I was miserable," Baker said. "I look back at my career and that's the one thing I wish I could have found a way to enjoy anything. You're the fat kid from Newark, you've done well—lighten up, relax, enjoy it."

The Aftermath

He survived his growing pains and learned from them.

"Now I know being different has made me successful in the business world," Baker said. "I also know what diplomacy means."

Baker owns a barbecue restaurant—Bubba's-Q Barbecue & Catering—in Avon, Ohio, near Cleveland. He also bottles his own Bubba's-Q barbecue sauce.

"I'm not just in the barbecue business, I have a patent, a very rare patent. We take a regular slab of ribs—not like McDonald's—a regular slab. We have created a patent where we remove the bones from a slab of ribs after they're cooked. What we're finding is a high population of women, people with dentures, people that are elderly—we de-bone baby back ribs."

Baker appeared on the reality TV show, *Shark Tank,* on December 6, 2013. (The show features budding entrepreneurs who present their ideas to a panel of investors.)

"We were the most watched episode ever. In one night we did over 7,000 orders because of that same march to a different beat of a drum. I married a woman who thought barbecue was good and was messy so she wouldn't eat it. I found a way to get her to eat it."

He found an investor on the show that night and business is good.

"There's not a day that doesn't go by when somebody doesn't contact my office from the U.K., Asia, Australia—they want to make my product where they are . . . I wouldn't do it because my patent is not in effect outside of the United States," Baker said.

The lessons Baker learned with the Lions and in the NFL are paying off today.

"I say to my son, I tell him that a mistake that a man makes is ordinary for men. When you learn from those mistakes, that's the mark of an extraordinary man," Baker said. "You've been through it and you've got to know invoke the forty-eight-hour rule. My partner Daymond John on *Shark Tank* we don't always agree on the direction of the new company. When something is said I write it down and I take advantage of the fact he's really busy. I won't say anything for two or three or four days, maybe a week. I know I have the upper-hand because I only have this one company. . . . I've learned to think it through, get over it."

In other words, Baker has learned when to keep his mouth shut.

"I think you write those things off to being young, to being inexperienced, not qualified to be a leader because you know when you become a leader you realize that guy already feels bad. You don't have to verbalize it," Baker said.

"That's how I became who I was, the mistakes I made in Detroit made me a better teammate that's why I ended up playing in the league thirteen years, I learned to internalize it. I didn't like losing," Baker said. "If you were not a guy that thinks you're equipped for losing being in Detroit was not a good place for you."

CHAPTER 4

ALEX KARRAS

Defensive tackle, 1958–1962, 1964–1970

The Game: November 8, 1970 vs. the New Orleans Saints at Tulane Stadium

NEW ORLEANS SAINTS 19, DETROIT LIONS 17

When Alex Karras died, the headline in the *Chicago Tribune* read: "Actor, also starred in NFL."

It had been so many years since he had played for the Detroit Lions that fans either forgot or didn't realize he had played, and played so well that he had the talent to get in the Pro Football Hall of Fame, although not enough fans in the right places.

Karras anchored the defensive line for twelve seasons over thirteen years with the Lions. He was an iron man of sorts, missing only one game due to injury. He was a cornerstone of the Fearsome Foursome in the 1960s, was named to four Pro Bowls and is a member of the NFL's All-Decade team of the 1960s.

Before the NFL he was the Outland Trophy winner at Iowa as the nation's top interior lineman.

He used to tell people, "I never graduated college, but I was only there for two terms—Truman's and Eisenhower's."

He was drafted 10th overall by the Lions in 1958 out of Iowa.

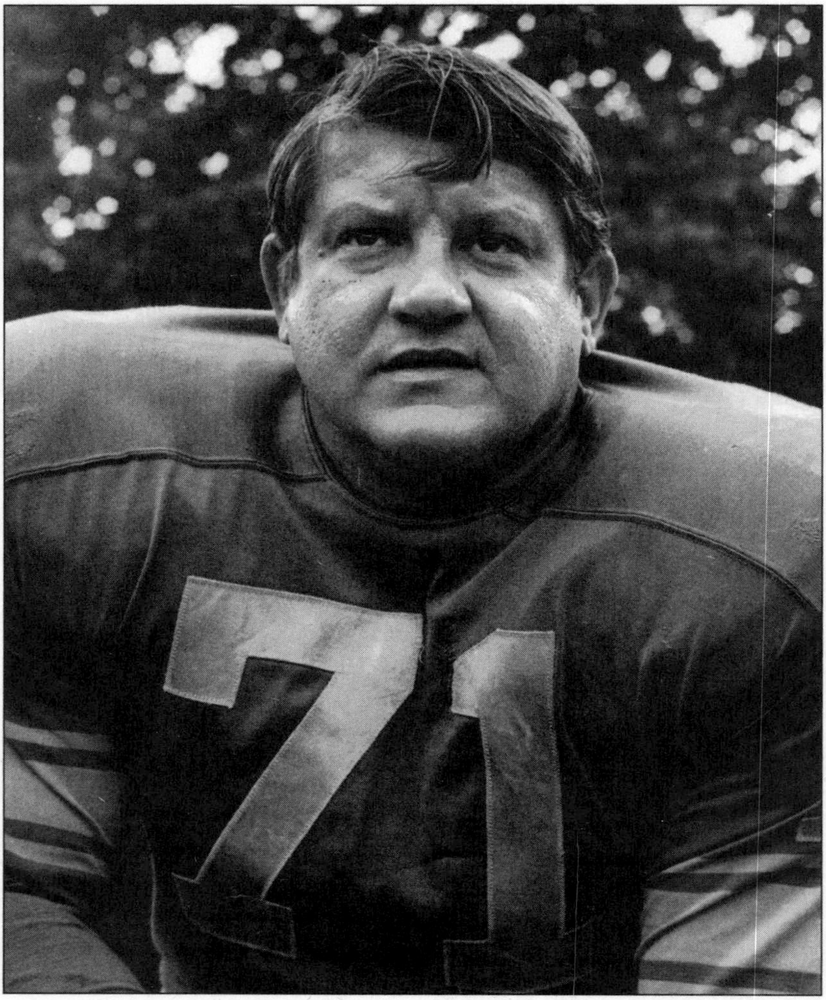

Alex Karras was a party waiting to happen off the field, but was all business on the field. *Photo courtesy of the Detroit Lions*

Karras once described his NFL draft-day experience as only he could (according to *USA Today*: "I made a collect call to the Lions after they drafted me and they wouldn't accept it").

In 1963, Karras was banned from the NFL for gambling. During his year off he became a pro wrestler who took on Dick the Bruiser among others.

After his NFL days, he was Mongo, the slow-witted thug under a 10-gallon hat who knocked out a horse in the movie, *Blazing Saddles*. It may be what he is most remembered for.

The Game

By Alex Karras and Others

And yet one of the most vivid memories for Alex Karras, who died on October 10, 2012, at age seventy-seven, was a home game against the hapless New Orleans Saints on November 8, 1970.

He was on the field when Tom Dempsey broke the NFL field goal mark, sending the football through the uprights with room to spare from 63 yards out.

This is how Karras described it to hosts Elliott Harris and David Spada in one of his final radio interviews before he died in 2012:

"My favorite moment was when Tom Dempsey, who was a very heavy-set, round kind of football player who didn't play much football other than kicking field goals. We were playing against them to make a long story short, he's going to try for a field goal. We say to each other, 'That's 60-something yards, we don't even have to rush that. We can get that without any problem at all.' Basically that was our attitude. Now the ball was snapped, he takes his time, when he hit the ball it sounds like a rocket went off. We all turned around, all the way around to watch it. It was going through the air like it was never going to stop. It went right [between the posts] and the crowd couldn't say a word. It was total quiet."

Karras, according to a *New York Daily News* story, turned to referee Jim Tunney and said, "You've got to be [bleeping] me."

Anyone who knew Karras knows that story. That includes his son George (who was named after George Plimpton, the author of *Paper Lion* which featured Alex Karras and his teammates).

"There was one I know, the Tom Dempsey game," George Karras said. "He didn't even rush.

"He literally said he heard the foot go boom. He said it was a boom like the sound of a wood block hitting the ball. He just went, 'OK, we're good, we're done. No way.'"

On the sideline at Tulane Stadium, linebacker Joe Schmidt heard the same thing. "It sounded almost like an explosion when he hit it," Schmidt told the *New York Daily News*. "That ball just kept going and going."

"It just had the feeling you get when everything is right," Dempsey told reporters. "You feel it the second you hit it."

Schmidt believes Karras could've batted it down if he had tried. "Hey, God bless the guy. He made it," Schmidt said. "It teaches you a lesson. You're never out of it. You always have a chance."

Hall of Fame tight end Charlie Sanders was on the field for the Lions that day.

"Nobody rushed, we thought it was a trick play. Sixty-three yards. Nobody rushed," Sanders said. "The next year they trade Dempsey to the Rams and if he makes a field goal the Lions could go to the playoffs and that [expletive] missed it."

Actually the whole situation was worse than it sounds.

Dempsey was born without toes on his right foot—his kicking foot—so he was wearing a specially designed $200 shoe that was square where the toes should be. Not everyone in the NFL thought it was fair that he could kick with that type of shoe including Karras.

When reporters asked Dempsey if he thought it was unfair, he said: "Unfair eh? How about you try kicking a 63-yard field goal to win it with two seconds left and you're wearing a square shoe, oh, yeah and no toes either."

Dempsey typically wasn't that good of a field-goal kicker. In that 1970 season, he kicked just five field goals in fifteen attempts.

The Saints were just in their fourth NFL season. They were 1–5–1 entering the game that was played on a clammy, overcast day at Tulane Stadium in New Orleans.

The Lions, who were 10-point favorites, had taken the 17–16 lead with an 18-yard field goal by Earl Morrall with just fourteen seconds left. The Lions thought they had won.

Then the Saints got within "field goal range" with two seconds remaining and with Dempsey's kick beat the Lions 19–17. It was one of two wins that season for the Saints who finished 2–11–1.

Dempsey's 63-yard kick broke the NFL record for field goals by seven yards.

His record was matched but not broken until Matt Prater, who was with the Broncos, kicked a 64-yard field goal on December 8. 2013. The next season Prater signed with the Lions.

"The adrenalin was working," Dempsey said the day after in an interview with the *New York Times*. "The snap was perfect, the ball was placed perfectly—and I had the strength. I'm still stunned today thinking about it. Tomorrow, I'll have to get my mind on the next game. But this is my day."

"I learned as a kid from my father that there was no such word as 'can't,'" he said in that interview. "He'd make me try everything, and I wouldn't be satisfied until I was good at everything I tried. And in high school my coach wouldn't let me feel different. I had a tendency to feel sorry for myself. But the coach would say, 'Stop feeling sorry for yourself. Come on, keep working.'"

To lose in such a fashion was a crusher.

"They won the game with a miracle," Lions coach Joe Schmidt told reporters.

"This is unbelievable. He could hit the ball again 200 times and I don't think he'd hit it that sweet again," said Lions kicker Errol Mann.

Oddly enough, a few weeks earlier Mann had predicted that someone in the NFL would kick a 60-yard field goal.

"There is a possibility of kicking it farther than 60 yards," Mann said in an October 21, 1970, *Detroit News* story. "That is if they have the wind from behind and a nice warm day. You need time to stride into it and a perfect snap and a perfect set.

"There will be a 60-yarder especially with the new artificial turf. When everybody gets it there will be standard surfaces—not a change in grass height from one field to another," Mann added.

In the game the Sunday before the miracle kick, Karras had sustained a concussion. Did he have a lingering reaction that day? Nothing has been said.

But in the November 1 loss to the Vikings, Karras said afterwards he "thought I was gonna die."

"I came staggering off the field and I told the team doctor that I thought I was going . . . that I was having a heart attack or something," Karras told the *Detroit News*.

"Everything was black. Scared? You bet I was scared. I never felt anything like that before in all my years of football. . . . My head kept ringing louder and louder and my vision got fuzzy until I couldn't see anything and came out of the game. I walked into the locker room but I don't remember how I got there."

The team doctors diagnosed him with a concussion, which is common these days. While concussions were certainly a part of the NFL generations ago, not much was said about them.

That game was one of the last for Karras, who was released following the last cutdown day after the 1971 training camp. In fact, he found out about his release while taping a Johnny Carson show. "That's how he found out the Lions had released him," George Karras said. "Everybody else knew before we did."

Karras, who was thirty-six at the time, had two years at $35,000 per year remaining on his contract. He fully expected to play in the 1971 season.

"I'm shocked, shocked as everybody else," he told reporters. "I had told Joe [Schmidt] I wasn't going to play hard in the preseason games. I felt I started coming on in the last two games. If I felt I couldn't go, then I would have understood it. But I felt I could do the job. My knee is better, my quickness is back. I can't understand it."

The fans missed him and so did his teammates.

"Honest to God he was a fun guy," Charlie Sanders said. "You could look at him and start laughing."

Sanders tells a story about being a rookie and being a little intimidated by Karras. They were on a bus one day on the way to a game, when Karras handed Sanders a picture of cute children and said they were his. Sanders told him what a lovely family he had. Then Karras hands him a photo of the ugliest woman imaginable and tells the rookie that's his wife. Sanders was a little stumped, but told Karras she was lovely. They got along fabulously after that.

When Karras returned to play in 1964 after being suspended in 1963 for gambling, he was asked to call a pre-game coin toss by officials. "I'm sorry, sir. I'm not permitted to gamble," Karras said according to an ESPN story detailing the top 10 sports suspensions of all time.

While Karras was a party-waiting-to-happen off the field, he was all business on it.

"There was no joking on the field, everyone was concerned for survival," Sanders said. "It was 'get him before he gets you.' We didn't have any rules. We weren't protected. Back in the day players used to say, 'Hit me in the head, don't go after my knees.' Because your knees were your survival. You welcomed a hit in the head, if you went for a guy's knees that a no-no because you were messing with my career."

Karras hated two things, everyone knew that.

"Rookies and kickers. Had no use for rookies until you proved you could play. And if there was one thing worse, it was kickers," Sanders told *Newsday* after Karras died. "These were the guys that would come in and be the heroes after all the blood, sweat, and tears from the other guys. Alex said they think they're kicking touchdowns and getting all the credit."

He especially hated highly paid rookies. In one case he said he determined in his own way that the youngster was indeed worth the money. "I threw him in the lake and, sure enough, he walked on water," Karras told the *Grand Rapids Press*.

Sanders remembers Karras fondly.

"He was just naturally a funny guy. You'd look at him just his stature, he had the wide shoulders, he had the small waist and the little skinny legs," Sanders told the *Oakland Press* after Karras died. "If you looked at him you'd start laughing and you would not associate this guy with being one of the meanest and toughest guys in the NFL, he didn't have that stature about him.

"So that in itself says a lot about his ability to accomplish the things he did. He didn't have the stature of Rosey Grier or Roger Brown. He was just a short, stocky kid that smoked a cigar," Sanders said.

Sanders, a Hall of Fame tight end, confirmed that Karras used to smoke cigars in the locker room showers. "He was the Godfather, that's what Godfathers do, I think. That was his symbol, was his cigar and of course the thick glasses and the big, burly chest, the bird legs, that was Alex," Sanders said.

(Oddly enough just before the Lions cut Karras in 1971, he had an audition for the role of the son-in-law in the movie, *The Godfather*.)

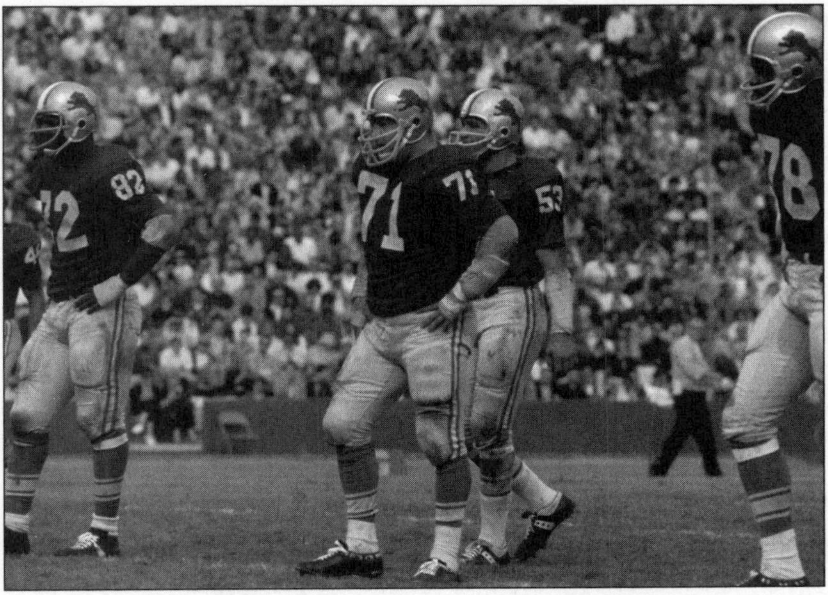

In twelve seasons with the Lions, Alex Karras missed only one game due to injury. *Photo courtesy of the Detroit Lions*

And yet for all his machismo, Karras had another side. In 1969 and 1970 he was an assistant coach in the Birmingham Bloomfield Football Little League for a team called the New York Jets. Perhaps an oddly named team considering Karras' occupation.

"I just wish we had a Joe Namath. Last year they were 0–7 and this year they'll probably be 0–7 again," Karras told the *Birmingham Eccentric.*

His oldest son Alex was on the team and he had three younger children. He was just helping out, he wasn't pushing his son into football. "I don't encourage and I don't discourage them. First of all they are very good boys. I enjoy teaching these kids. I get a real kick out of it," Karras said.

It was a different NFL back then, but still Sanders can't quite explain how Karras could excel being so under-sized. It was not his work in the weight room.

"Alex never lifted weights, Alex just smoked cigars and drank beer," Sanders said.

He was 6-foot-2 with a playing weight around 250. Someone once characterized his style of play as that of an "angry washerwoman."

"I was a little different than most guys at my position. I wasn't as big," he told the *Des Moines Register* in a 1977 interview. "The guys now don't play the lateral game I did. I'd run around the opposition, not through them. Linemen today weigh 290 and can lift houses. They play a different game, but they're damn good."

Wayne Walker and Karras were Lions rookies in 1958 and Walker had a special appreciation for Karras.

"Alex was probably the most individual man/football player ever," Walker told *USA Today* after Karras died. "He was just so original. There was no one like him before and there won't be anyone like him after. He had this Jackie Gleason–type body and, God, he could really play. He could really play. He threw offensive linemen around."

In his obituary in the *New York Times*, Karras was described as "an especially versatile pass rusher, known around the league for his combination of strength, speed and caginess. His furious approach—Plimpton described it as a 'savage, bustling style of attack' earned him the nickname the Mad Duck. His teammates often referred to him as 'Mr. Twinkletoes.'"

Plimpton got to know Karras when the author wrote *Paper Lion* after spending a training camp with the Detroit Lions in an effort to get playing time as a quarterback in one of the Lions' preseason games.

The book opened the doors of an NFL team at training camp back then and was eventually turned into a movie. Alan Alda played Plimpton and Alex Karras played himself.

Plimpton, who established "participatory journalism" in the 1960s, got the story behind the closed doors of the locker room. While Plimpton was in training camp with the Lions in 1963,

Karras had been banned. But Plimpton had heard all the stories and then met Karras the next season when he was back in action.

Plimpton described Karras this way in the book: "His torso was enormous. In his self-deprecatory manner he used to say that if the rest of him was in proper proportion to his torso he'd be eight feet tall. On the field he ran, his teammates said of him like a 'mad duck' but they used to swear softly thinking of his ability."

When Karras' acting career took off, his teammates must have seen it coming. In the dining room or wherever players would gather, Karras used to put on skits and monologues. If not enough men were paying attention, he'd bang his water glass until they did.

Plimpton wrote in detail about some of these monologues.

"It was Karras' fantasy that he had lived a succession of different lives—stretching far back into the past. He had been, among other things an aide-de-camp to both General Washington and Adolf Hitler," Plimpton wrote.

When Karras missed the 1963 season, he was replaced by Floyd Peters, who had big shoes to fill.

What the teammates likely didn't miss was one of Karras' pre-game habits—he got violently ill before each game.

"Just as [Coach] George Wilson tells us to go out there and rock them, out in the can we'll hear Alex lose his lunch. Sure. And then in five minutes he'll out there on the field making the poor fellow from Philadelphia opposite him pay for it," teammate Gary Lowe was quoted in *Paper Lion*.

Karras was on *Monday Night Football* for three seasons (1974–76) along with Howard Cosell and Frank Gifford. In a YouTube clip from the intro to an October 18, 1976, game with the Patriots playing the Jets coached by Lou Holtz, Karras sings a fight song inspired by Holtz's college background at North Carolina State.

Cosell cracked up.

Karras used to say: "I'm the bridge between Howard Cosell and Frank Gifford. I'm there to have a little fun."

It was a long successful career for the Indiana native who was drafted in the first round in 1958, the year after the Lions had won the National Championship in 1957—their third in six years.

"When you have Bobby Layne at quarterback you know you have some kind of great team," Karras said in that final radio interview. "To me he was the best quarterback I've ever seen play football. I was really, really up for it when they said you can go there and play for Detroit. We had some ball club and it was a together ball club. We all liked each other which was really good. We played as we played and we won."

The Aftermath

Many younger NFL fans didn't even know that Karras played in the NFL.

They knew him as George Papadapolis from the TV show *Webster*.

"Acting is hard work but it sure as hell beats playing professional football," Karras once said.

In his CNN obit his family said he had always dreamed of being an actor. They said he got a boost when Lucille Ball took him under her wing and let him train in small parts.

He had small roles on several television shows and then he broke out on the big screen with roles in *Porky's* and *Victor, Victoria*.

He's probably most famous for playing Mongo with his famous line: "Mongo only pawn in the game of life."

In TV movies he played a backwoods weight lifter in *The 500-Pound Jerk* and the husband of Babe Didrikson Zaharias in *Babe*. His wife, Susan Clark, played Babe.

Karras also co-wrote autobiographies *Even Big Guys Cry* and *Alex Karras: My Life in Football, Television, and Movies*. He also wrote a novel, *Tuesday Night Football*, based on his experiences on *Monday Night Football.*

When he died, Lions team president Tom Lewand said: "While his legacy reached far beyond the gridiron, we always will fondly remember Alex as one of our own and also as one of the best to ever wear the Honolulu blue and silver."

The obit from *Sports Illustrated* exhibited his joy for life: "One of the fiercest pass rushers of his day, Karras didn't look the part. At 6–2 and 248 pounds he was undersized at tackle—an *SI* story on him was headlined 'A Giant Midget Among Giant Men.' (Karras compensated with a nimbleness that earned him the nickname Mr. Twinkletoes.) He also wore thick, horn-rimmed glasses that, as George Plimpton noted, gave Karras 'a benign, owl-like bearing.' That mien suited him well after his twelve seasons with the Lions, during which he was a three-time All-Pro.

His turns as an actor are memorable. But the role in which Karras shone brightest was that of himself. With his quick wit and affability, he cracked up Johnny Carson, spent three years in the *Monday Night Football* booth, slung insults on Dean Martin's roasts and was the ideal game-show guest. (On *Match Game* he once winged a wrestling demonstration with a contestant who grappled professionally as Lola Kiss, the Kiss of Death from Transylvania.)"

Karras was diagnosed with dementia at age seventy. He joined a lawsuit against the NFL accusing the league of failing to warn players about long-term brain damage from concussions. He died after fighting kidney disease, heart disease, dementia, and stomach cancer.

When he died his family released this statement: "Alex was known to family and friends as a gentle, loving, generous man who loved gardening and preparing Greek and Italian feasts."

Such a full life.

Chapter 5

DOUG ENGLISH

Defensive tackle, 1975–1979, 1981–1985

The Game: November 23, 1978 vs. the Denver Broncos at the Pontiac Silverdome

DETROIT LIONS 17, DENVER BRONCOS 14

Doug English hasn't played football since 1985 when he suffered a ruptured disc and was forced to retire from the Detroit Lions.

Not surprisingly, the former defensive tackle is still a fan of the game.

Even though he lives on a ranch near Austin, Texas, he tries to watch the Detroit Lions play when he gets a chance.

He loved the defensive line in 2014. Not just the players, but the coaches.

"I really like those guys and I love their coach Jim Washburn. I like both coaches. Kris [Kocurek] is super good and he's learning from the best. He's in such a good position as a young guy."

English said that Jim Washburn reminds him of Floyd Peters, the Lions defensive coordinator who built the Silver Rush, the Lions' defensive line that dominated in the late 1970s and early 1980s.

"Probably about seven or eight years ago, I'm watching *Monday Night Football*, I don't watch a lot of football but I had it on,"

Doug English, a four-time Pro Bowler, says he owes everything to his coaches through the years. *Photo courtesy of the Detroit Lions*

English said. "I noticed the Philadelphia Eagles defensive ends are in track stances, wide out, aimed in and these guys are coming after the passer like I haven't seen since we did.

"Young kids will come to me or Texas kids or some young rookie, and ask, 'Will you help me with the pass rush?' One of the first things I do, if you and I were in a race, track, what's your absolute best get-off stance. That's a track stance, that's it that's your pass-rush stance.

"Whatever moves you the fastest, get in that stance. None of this perfect form stuff—get your ass up, head down. So I look up and these guys (the Eagles) were in track stances, out wide and coming around the corner. That quarterback could hardly set his feet and he was getting hit. . . . I was watching and I thought I've got to find out who that coach is.

"I look it up and it's Jim Washburn. So his name is in my head.

"So I'm up here [at Lions practice] last year and watching our line. They introduced me to the defensive line coach. I'm like a kid, 'You're Jim Washburn, I'm grabbing him.' He's literally knocking my hands off (He demonstrates, moving his long arms like two windmills). I said,'You don't understand I've been waiting to meet you for a long time.' He's great."

"Great" is a word used to describe English, who played ten seasons for the Detroit Lions from 1975 to 1985, taking 1980 off to go back home to Texas and work in the oil business. He was drafted in the second round out of the University of Texas.

When he was inducted into the College Football Hall of Fame in 2011, the Detroit writers who had covered his playing days in Detroit chipped in with kind words in a story on TexasSports.com.

"Doug English made such an impression on Detroit that twenty-five years later he is still remembered," said former *Detroit News* beat writer Mike O'Hara. "I will use the words of his former coach, Monte Clark, to describe him: 'Doug English is a cut above the guys who usually came through as professional football players.' He was a great player, and a great guy. When they named an all-time Detroit Lions team for their 75th anniversary, Doug was on it."

Former *Detroit News* columnist Jerry Green said: "First of all, he was a human being. He was a great person as well as a great football player. We would go to dinner together once a year, and would talk about everything and anything except football. He had manifold interests. I really appreciated him. He was a wonderful pro."

English, who played at 6-foot-5 and 255 pounds, was a four-time Pro Bowl selection (1979, 1982–84) and finished his career with 59 sacks, still sixth on the Lions' all-time sacks list.

Sacks were a big reason for making the Thanksgiving game in 1978 his most memorable.

The Game

By Doug English

It was my fourth year, Thanksgiving game. We had a new staff and I had a new coach, Floyd Peters. He liked us. He really emphasized aggressive defense and aggressive defensive line play. We brought in Bubba (Al "Bubba" Baker) the top-round choice. We rocked along, we were doing pretty good and then Thanksgiving Day we had the Denver Broncos who were on track to go to the Super Bowl.

We had ten or twelve sacks that day, I had four. It was sort of my breakout game as a Lion. And it's Thanksgiving Day, which back then not all games were on TV. All my family and friends in Texas were able to see the game.

That's two things—it was a breakout game and all my family and friends got to see the game. Three, there is something special about Thanksgiving Day. Detroit Lions on Thanksgiving Day is a very, very special game. I didn't realize it until we came up for Thanksgiving—actually my wife and I and kids came up and we had Thanksgiving with actor Tim Allen, who's a super guy and good friend. We all went to the game together, we had a little suite, I remember leaning out of that suite—it was still in the Silverdome—looking out and around and thinking it wasn't smoky, back then they allowed smoking. It wasn't smoky, it was families. There weren't a bunch of drunks coming off the shifts (at the auto plants), it was just a special day. I was like "God, yeah that's it, I can smell it."

It's a special day. Greg Morton—he played at Dallas, backed up at Dallas, and got traded to Denver—was their quarterback. It was the game our D-line came together and started doing real well.

My coach used to say sacks come in bunches. That was my day.

That was the standout game.

We won. I think it was like 17–14 even though Denver had been favored.

It's an advantage to play for Detroit on Thanksgiving Day because it's a short week and you don't have to travel. So really it maximizes that you don't have to travel, it really cuts into your week if you have to travel for Thanksgiving, especially if it's two time zones. You travel two days early, so basically you have one day home and you have to take off.

Also it's a special day, Thanksgiving. Thanksgiving Day was always good for us, even in the bad years we'd win on Thanksgiving. I love that game.

***

The Lions' defense that day held the Broncos, who were 8–4 entering the game, to 233 net yards. The win boosted the Lions' record to an ugly 5–8.

The NFL didn't keep official stats on sacks until 1982, but English said they had a coach who counted them himself.

Other Memorable Moments

English's best season was in 1983 when he had 13 sacks. That year the Lions won the NFC Central with a 9–7 record and lost to the 49ers 24–23 in the divisional round.

English proved the man who first recruited him to play at the University of Texas correct. That was the late R.M. Patterson.

"He was a lanky, tall fellow that ran hard and worked hard to get to the football," Patterson remembered during English's senior year with the Longhorns, according to TexasSports.com. "I thought someday he might be a 6–5, 260 pound lineman with tremendous potential."

Bingo.

"I liked what I saw in every way," Patterson said then. "He just came from an all-American family. You know any person who has great ability will be a natural leader. But when you get a real exceptional person with a great attitude as well, you'll almost always find good results, whether it's in football, or in any aspect of life."

English was the Longhorns' team captain and most valuable player in 1974. He was a consensus All-American his senior season and was a two-time all–Southwest Conference selection at Texas in 1973 and 1974.

English has given back to the community and has long been involved in research for spinal cord and traumatic brain injuries. He is the founder and president of the Lone Star Paralysis Foundation whose mission is to "work ourselves out of business."

Buried in his resume is his role in the 1990 movie *Big Bad John* based on the Jimmy Dean song of the same name. English played the role of Big Bad John Tyler while Dean and Ned Beatty had the leading roles.

"I started and sold three companies since I got out of football," English said. "I've never had a boss other than a coach. Now I have a fourth company and I'm back in football. I call it the 'Power Drive.'" It's a training tool for football players that reinforces power hip flexion. English got the idea for it when he was rolling bags of feed for his longhorn cattle on his ranch.

The motion mimics that of a defensive lineman who needs his posterior up and head down as he pushes forward. The tool is dedicated to teaching and strengthening perfect form at the point of attack. It's more popular at the college level. He's sold four to the University of Michigan.

His playing days are long gone, but in a small way now Doug English is still involved in the game. Over the years, he's always maintained a close relationship with the Lions' organization. Fans, even those who weren't old enough to see him play, know him or know of him.

In February 2015, he was inducted into the Michigan Sports Hall of Fame with a distinguished class that included former Red Wings center Sergei Fedorov and Michigan State men's basketball coach Tom Izzo.

English's acceptance speech was short that night. His words offer a glimpse into the man that he is these days.

"To the Detroit Lions, thank you for all you've done for me since I was twenty-one years old.

"The inductees, today what an honor. My first thought was there must be a mistake, I can't be on the same dais with these folks. Congratulations to all of you, you're spectacular, thank you.

"If I had to get down to the most important point that I can make it's that every good thing that's happened to me in my life is not something I did it's as a result of great coaches. [He pointed to Izzo and the other coaches in the audience and said, 'God bless you.'] Coaches make athletes, good coaches, great coaches make great athletes that's the way it works. You take one coach out of my career and somebody else is standing here with this microphone in their hands. I just want to say my life has been blessed by mentors and coaches, they come in all shapes—it's not just guys in polyester shorts and a whistle. My wife's a pretty good coach, [he introduced his wife Clare]. My mother and my father were excellent coaches. My high school coaches, college, I had the right coach in my life every step of the way and without any one of those people things could have turned out in a different way. I'm a very, very lucky man. I received the help I needed when I needed it and the inspiration I needed when I needed it. And now my job, and I believe everyone will agree with this, is to continue to pass those blessings on."

There you go.

That is Doug English from the heart.

Chapter 6

CHARLIE SANDERS

Tight end, 1968–1977

The Game: November 26, 1970 vs. the Oakland Raiders at Tiger Stadium

DETROIT LIONS 28, OAKLAND RAIDERS 14

Charlie Sanders knew the Detroit Lions, perhaps better than anyone.

After retirement, he worked as a television analyst and assistant coach for years before moving into the Lions' personnel office where he worked until months before his death on July 2, 2015.

Sanders, who was inducted into the Pro Football Hall of Fame in 2007, knew football and he knew the Lions after spending forty-three years with the organization.

So when he said the 1970 team was the best Lions team ever, trust him.

"Everything gelled, everything came together. It was good," Sanders said in an interview in March 2015, four months before his death.

Greg Landry was the quarterback. Two future Hall of Famers started at cornerback—Lem Barney and Dick LeBeau. Mel Farr was the running back and Sanders was the tight end.

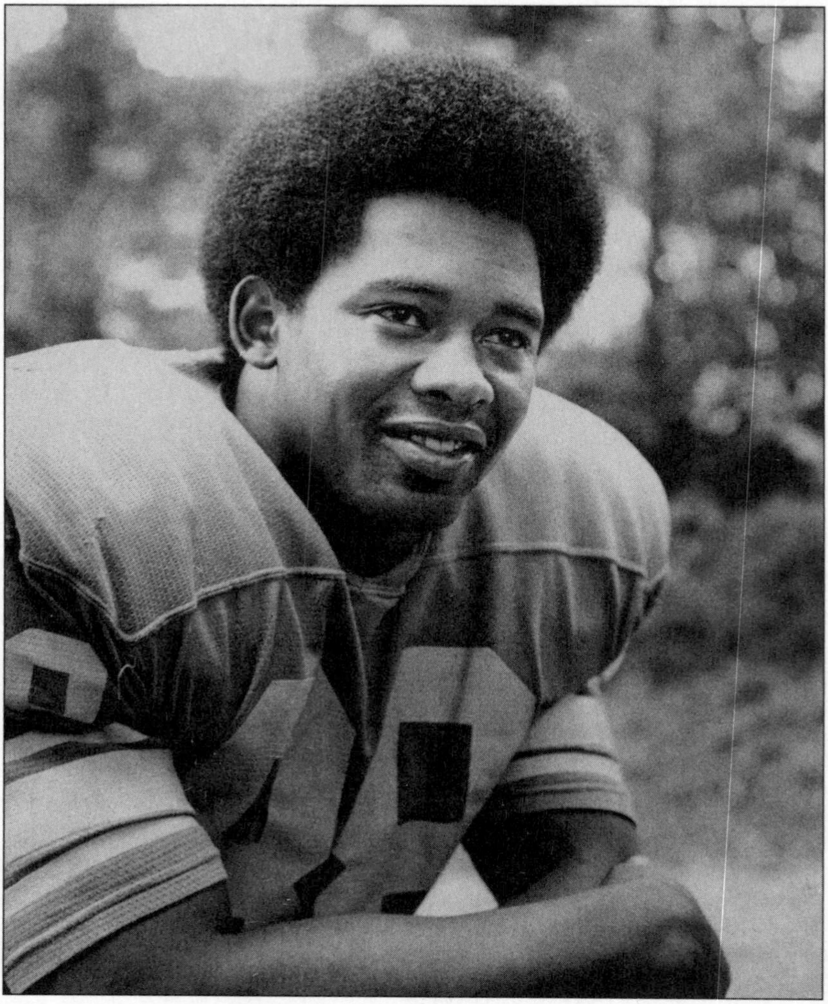

Hall of Famer Charlie Sanders is routinely considered the Lions' best tight end ever. *Photo courtesy of the Detroit Lions*

They were coached by Hall of Famer Joe Schmidt.

Not a bad roster.

"It was a group of old men, guys that had been around, had come together. You hear about people jelling it was a prime example of teams jelling at the right time," Sanders said. "The young guys stepped it up, the old guys were on their last legs but they had that one year left in them. Everything seemed to fall into place for us. I think after that year, that was the year we had a chance I think to start establishing a dynasty."

Wow, those are some powerful words.

They finished the season 10–4 and went on to face Dallas in the playoffs. They lost 5–0 in a game that still seemed to gnaw at Sanders. They didn't know it at the time, but it was their one shot at glory.

"We did not replace, we let the team get old and we had to replace too many guys at too many positions. Over the course of the years they let everybody get old," Sanders said. "That was the 1970s, half the team didn't return after that."

That Thanksgiving game was crucial to the season.

With the win they boosted their record to 7–4. They had beaten the San Francisco 49ers the previous Sunday, then went on to win the final three games too. They finished the season at 10–4, good enough for second (to the Vikings) in the NFC Central.

So it's no wonder that Sanders' most memorable game was on Thanksgiving in 1970.

The Game

By Charlie Sanders

It would have to be the 1970 Thanksgiving game, I had a game that I think people said, "Who is this guy?" And my career just kind of continued from there. It was a memorable game, it was a nationally televised game. Of course, back in those days we didn't get on television too often.

All I remember is we were down 14–0 and I ended up with two touchdowns in that game and a memorable catch that people still refer to as "The Catch." We won and we went on to the playoffs and that was a big game for us as a team and for us as an organization because we got to the playoffs.

You always listen to your coaches, it was a catch that I really didn't think I would catch it, it was one of those "You know what let's make it look a good catch." There was no way I figured I was going to make this catch, so I'll make it look good, I'll dive for it. I dove for it, put my hands out there, the ball hits and I'm hitting the ground and just missing the goal post—back then the goal post was only a yard off the goal line.

If you get a close up of it you can actually see the ball was being caught with my fingernails. I don't even know how it happened. That would probably be the most memorable game and the most memorable play I had in my entire career.

I talked with John Madden, who was the Raiders' coach that day, years later and he remembers that game, too.

It was a just a simple post pattern and quarterback Greg Landry called an option. I had an option to run a post or corner route we just locked on and he found me . . . Again, I had no idea (n)or did I expect to make that catch.

If you actually look at it you can actually see my fingernails gripping the ball. It didn't hit in the palm of my hand, it was being gripped by my fingernails. If you look at that, if you are teaching technique, that would not be the technique.

At that point in time it was destined to be my day. That tied the game and then I had another touchdown in the corner that put us ahead. We went on to win that game, we won the last five games of the season and went to the playoffs.

We ended up playing Dallas in the playoffs—that was the 5–0 loss.

To this day that was the best team Detroit ever had, bar none.

Best team Detroit's ever had. We lost to Dallas and they went on to win the Super Bowl. That was the best team I've been associated with playing or coaching.

"Sanders' great catches were the big reason we lost," Madden told the Associated Press after that Thanksgiving game.

The diving catch was for 20 yards while the touchdown that gave the Lions the lead was a six-yard leaping catch in the north corner of the end zone.

While that Thanksgiving game stands out in Sanders' mind, he has never forgotten the playoff game that season when they lost to the Cowboys 5–0.

"We ended up with a safety against us. The game was being played between the 20-yard lines, everything was happening between the 20s, no one could get in the end zone," Sanders said. "We ended up with a safety on us. The game was 2–0 for the majority of the game. Later on, they kicked a field goal and made it 5–0.

"The last series they pulled Greg Landry and put Bill Munson in. That was a controversy there over the change. Munson marched us right down the field on the last series. He threw a pass to Earl McCullouch. We questioned if it should have been caught—it was one of those. I still see it. It went off his fingertips and hit another guy in the chest. At that point on the field, I dropped to my knees and said, 'Oh no' and just collapsed right there on the field. I knew that was the game. That stayed with me for a long time, still to this day."

At that point the Lions had not won a playoff since 1957. Of course no one knew, but they wouldn't win another until 1991.

It was Sanders' only career playoff game. No wonder it haunted him for years.

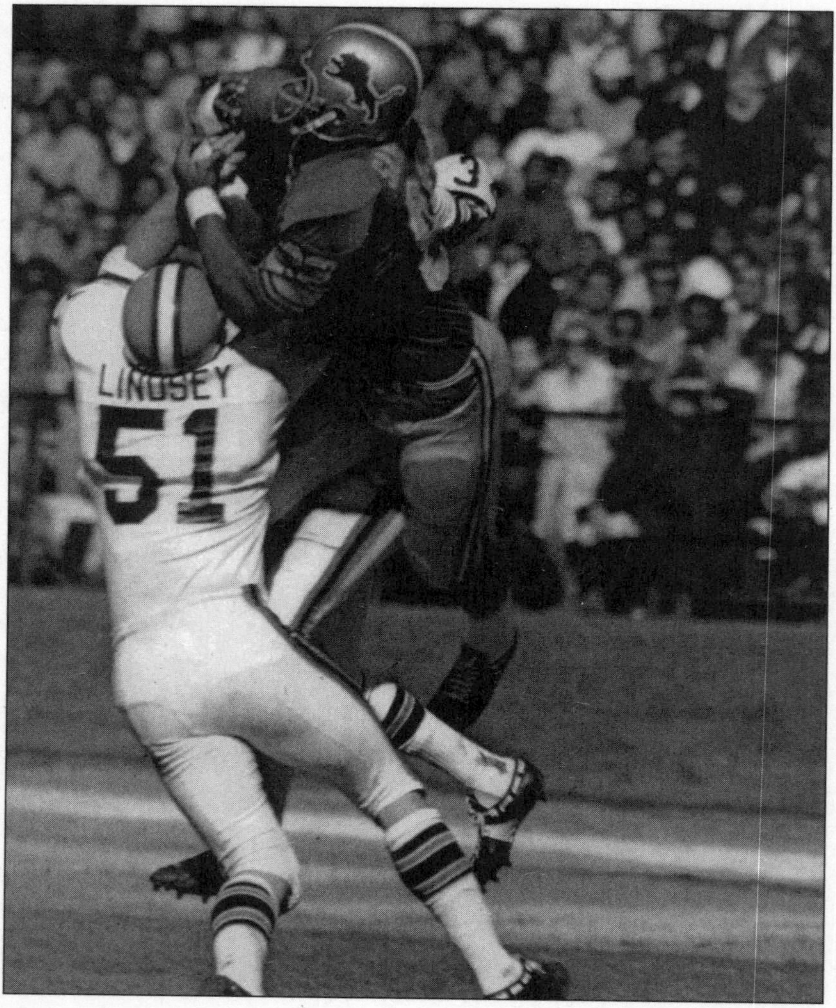

Charlie Sanders out jumps two Cleveland defenders for another pass reception. *Photo courtesy of the Detroit Lions*

Other Memorable Moments

Those Thanksgiving touchdowns were just two of Sanders' 31 career touchdowns and 336 career receptions. The 336 career receptions set a franchise record that would stand for twenty years until broken by wide receiver Herman Moore in 1996.

No wonder Sanders was a seven-time Pro Bowl selection (1968, 1969, 1970, 1971, 1974, 1975, and 1976). Obviously he was consistent over the course of his career, which started when he was drafted in the third round out of Minnesota by the Lions. He was the Lions' starting tight end for ten seasons.

He was also first team All-Pro in 1970 and 1971. And he was named to the NFL's 1970s All-Decade team and the Lions' 75th anniversary team.

A tight end can't be judged just on statistics. Sanders was also known for his superior blocking, during an era when tight ends blocked more than they do now. Sanders was an athlete who played basketball and football at Minnesota, so as a rookie he was the Lions' secret weapon. He just didn't stay a secret that long.

He's widely regarded as the best Lions' tight end of all time.

That Thanksgiving game wasn't the greatest game of his career based just on numbers. His best game statistically came as a rookie, on December 15, 1968, when he had 10 catches for 133 yards against the Washington Redskins. He went on to become the only rookie to earn a Pro Bowl selection that season.

Teammate Doug English, a defensive tackle, remembers being intimidated by Sanders until he got to know him.

English remembers Sanders rocking back and forth on the stool by his locker in the days leading up to each game while smoking a cigarette and drinking coffee.

Sanders didn't deny this. He said back then everybody smoked.

"Coaches smoked on the sidelines, believe it or not. That shows how ignorant we were. In 1977 I got my cigarette from the doctor who operated on my knee right in the hospital. He reached down and got one out of his shirt pocket," Sanders said.

This was about the time information had been released that smoking was damaging to the lungs.

"So the younger guys were coming in and looking at us, 'These guys are smoking.' Half the team smoked," Sanders said.

"My last meal was Saturday night. I didn't eat from Saturday to Monday. I was very difficult to be around. You didn't want to be around me pre-game, you didn't want to be around me at all. I was very involved in my rituals.

"I didn't have any friends at that time on the team or off the team. You didn't want to be around me. I was not a nice person. I laugh at my career. I was not a nice guy. I had friends who would speak [to opponents]. I did not treat you that way, neither would I recognize you as a friend. I recognized numbers. I didn't want to know your name. After a game I went my way and before a game I didn't want to know you. You were a person who was trying to prevent me from the best I could be."

To those who knew Sanders in recent years until his death—even casually—this is almost hard to believe. He was the friendly guy strolling the halls of the Lions' practice facility. He had a word for everyone on the days he went out on the field to watch practice.

But if Sanders said it, it's the truth.

"I remember being at chapel service once. I had this thing against a guy—we took turns trying to inflict pain on each other. I was at the chapel service before the game and I broke out crying because here I was listening to the chaplain talk about God and I was sitting there figuring out how I was going to try to kill this guy. I just broke down crying.

"This is a part of the game a lot of people don't understand. When they look at ball players they can't figure out how this guy can do this when he's gotten out of a game that is so violent. I think the difference is the game is more physical, the mindset is a lot different.

"It was a war it was not a game. It was a war. When you went through that tunnel that was the best you were going to feel that day. You didn't know why, when or wherever, but you knew you were not going to come back the same physically or mentally after the game," Sanders said.

"In order for you to be consistent in that thinking, it was hard to take your foot off the gas or to change that mindset. What happens is after the game is over with, a lot of players have to figure out who they are. Many of us players would try to bring God and Christianity into the game and at the same time you're fighting a war," he said.

"Football was no game. You get out of the game you try to figure out who you are. Are you the Christian you were striving to be while you were playing the game? You don't know . . . I think a lot of ball players they think back, they went through so much mentally it was hard for them to adjust to life after," Sanders said.

He said he didn't understand how Christianity and football could mix until he was fifty years old.

In the era he played in, there were no rules. There were no concussion tests. Hits to the head? Totally allowed.

"You want to be this guy I'd try to knock your head off, I'd try to break your leg," Sanders said. "We didn't have any rules. It was a game of survival."

Today there are rules against hitting a guy in the head.

"The only rule we had, that showed lack of respect if you went at a guy's knees. We'd say hit me in the head, don't go after my knees. Because that was our only source of survival. You don't have knees you can't run, you can't run you can't play. That was the rule of thumb you want to end a guy's career you go after his knee.

"That was the one rule that dictated, once you passed that rule you were dirty. You were considered dirty," Sanders said. "I went after a few guys' heads and hit a few guys' knees whenever it presented itself. Those were the rules we played under. Basically we didn't have any."

His pre-game ritual started days before kickoff.

"The opponent, the game, the play. I could tell you after the game every play that I ran, everything I did on every play," Sanders said. "It was in my mind before I could try to determine what I was going to do on each play. You find yourself playing the game two or three times in the course of two days. With that hyperventilating and nervousness you didn't eat."

In his rookie year he arrived at camp weighing 235 (he's 6-foot-4) and ended the season at 207 pounds. During the season on a good day he would weigh 215.

"Matter of fact Joe Schmidt wouldn't let me practice because I was losing weight. I couldn't eat, I'd get so nervous I couldn't hold food down," Sanders said. "A lot of guys I'd go out to the Pro Bowl, they'd look at me. Man, I wore big pads. I had a lot of compromised pads that were made by the trainer. I had the big Fiberglas thigh pads that made your legs look bigger. You wore the big lineman shoulder pads to make your shoulders look broader. You put on a couple pair of socks up top to make your calves look bigger.

"I would try to say I was sick before I got here so I lost a few pounds. You didn't want them to know this is all I weighed. Herman Moore, a wide receiver, weighed more than I did," Sanders said.

Maybe it was the cigarettes.

"Before the game I'd drink a cup of coffee and have a cigarette. At halftime I'd light up a cigarette," Sanders said. "It's crazy now, nobody smokes. Back in the day everybody smoked—coaches, general managers, players, everybody smoked, it was accepted."

He vividly remembers his teammate Alex Karras who smoked cigars.

"He was a funny man, I enjoyed it. He liked me because I made him laugh. I enjoyed being around him," Sanders said.

The Aftermath

One reason Sanders retired when he did was his bad knee.

He hung on for years, knowing a knee replacement was inevitable. He finally went through with it in February 2015.

"Not a lot of people know about it, from a medical standpoint it's rarely heard of. What happened somewhere during the course of those years a tumor developed in the knee," Sanders said.

It was cancer. The next step for the doctors was to determine where in his body the cancer had originated. Early indications were that it had not spread.

Prior to the surgery, his knee presented itself differently.

"Now all of a sudden I'm having problems with my knee I hadn't had before, the doctor drained it and did an MRI and he didn't like the way things looked. From the MRI he basically figured out there were some 'hot spots' that should not have been there," Sanders explained about a month after the surgery.

"Usually you get cancer it comes from somewhere else, it usually metastasizes in one of the other organs. This went right to my knee and the only explanation they had is that it went to the weakest source in my body and thank God it was the knee that needed to be replaced instead of the pancreas," Sanders said. "It didn't touch anything. It traveled throughout my whole body and said let's make a home in this knee he's got to replace."

He remained upbeat although a month after surgery he was getting antsy about getting back to work as the Lions' assistant director of pro personnel. But in the next few months the cancer was found to have spread. While Sanders battled—just like he had on the football field—he was no match for lung cancer. He was sixty-eight when he died.

Sanders had quickly become a fan of coach Jim Caldwell, who led the Lions to an 11–5 record in his first season in 2014.

"He reminds me so much of Joe Schmidt. I tell people with a guy like that you know where to find him. They say, 'What do you mean?' I said because he's the same guy on the field, off the field, wherever he is, that's who he is," Sanders said. "There's nothing phony about him. I think that's why he's had so much success wherever he's gone it's because the players trust him, and he allows the players to earn that trust. That may have been some of the problem we've had in the past. . . . He is how he is. I would have loved to play for him."

When Sanders was not working, he was involved in charity work.

In recent years he was involved in heart screen tests for high school age athletes. It's called "Have a Heart Save a Life" and is part of the Charlie Sanders Foundation (haveaheartsavealife.org).

He was not just lending his name; this was something that was important to him.

"I was sitting watching television one night a few years ago and the Wes Leonard story popped up, they showed the clips of the winning basket and him collapsing," Sanders said.

Leonard was a sixteen-year-old high school basketball player from Fennville, Michigan, who died of cardiac arrest due to dilated cardiomyopathy—an enlarged heart—after hitting the game-winning shot.

"I'm sitting there and I'm older now and everything I got after the age of sixty is icing on the cake. I'm sitting there saying you know there's something not right about this, the fact that this is probably the greatest moment in this kid's life and he only had a matter of seconds to realize it. And there was something that wasn't fair about it and it's something that could have been prevented if the kid had a heart screen. It stuck with me and stuck with me that the kid never had a chance," said Sanders, who was the father of nine children with his ex-wife Georgianna.

A year or so later, it was still on his mind.

"I happened to be going to Lansing to speak to the house of representatives on concussions and I started telling Bill Keenist (the Lions senior vice president of communications) the story about Wes Leonard and I look over and Bill Keenist is crying," Sanders said.

Keenist's son Chris, a college football player, was discovered to have a similar condition but it was caught in time. Still the Keenist family lived through a harrowing few months.

"We're talking about kids that are dying and they're dying with the understanding they're participating in the one thing that God put every child here to do and that is to play. We as parents don't give them that opportunity to do that. Kids trust us. The last thing they think about is their heart health . . . I have nine kids. I never thought about my kids having a heart attack because they're young. Most parents are in the same mindset, he's young so he's healthy," Sanders said

Heart screenings can determine if a young athlete is at risk. The problem is that screenings can be expensive.

"The insurance and medical profession has priced it to the point where financially it's almost impossible to do for the low income families. That's really what has to be addressed, those are the kind of families that have to be reached," Sanders said.

Royal Oak Beaumont Hospital in suburban Detroit had started a program for healthy heart checks, so Sanders got involved.

"Last year we saved a young lady's life. Matter of fact she is the poster child for the program. Her dad heard about the heart screening. She was a cheerleader, she had a routine physical and passed. Her dad took her for a heart check and two weeks later she was getting a heart transplant. It was so bad they rushed her right to the University of Michigan Hospital in Ann Arbor."

Sanders raised money for the healthy heart checks with a celebrity-laden golf outing each year.

"This is the fourth year of the golf outing. It's been very, very successful and in the meantime we've saved some lives," Sanders said.

He pointed out recent *Wall Street Journal* articles that discuss whether the NCAA should demand that every student athlete have a heart screen.

That's fine but Sanders thought that was too late. He wanted to see a more universal approach for heart screens for younger athletes.

"We're playing Russian roulette with our kids," Sanders said.

It's just one of the causes that Sanders had taken an interest in over the years and showed what kind of person he was.

When he was inducted into the Pro Football Hall of Fame, Lions owner the late William Clay Ford made the introduction:

"Charlie is what you look for today in a tight end. He was a pioneer at that position. You knew he was Hall of Fame material. He looked that way right off the bat. He stood out. He had the speed, he had the hands for it, and he gave up his body. He was a devastating blocker. As far as setting a prototype example, Charlie was it.

"Charlie had a presence about him the opposition was aware of. He never bothered with the team meal. He had a habit of making these awful looking milkshakes. I'm calling it a milkshake. I think I'm being kind. I'm not sure what it was. But whatever it was, he was able to give his top performance every time.

"He was always so sure handed that he caught things in stride. You couldn't stop him. He was a freight train. You couldn't have a better example of the mental attitude and the physical attitude that he brought to the game.

"It was as great an honor for me to be asked by Charlie to be his presenter as it was for him to be elected to the Hall of Fame. We really chatted about it quite casually, but we kind of hemmed and hawed around a little bit. Finally it dawned on me that, gee, he'd like me to be his presenter, and I can't think of anything nicer.

"It can't get much better than being elected to the Hall of Fame. It represents the pinnacle of a career, and nobody can take that away from you. It's great," Ford said.

Sanders said that being elected to the Pro Football Hall of Fame changed everything.

"It actually saved my life to be honest with you. It gave me identity, it gave me a sense of obligation to always give to society, everything. You go through life trying to figure out who you are, how you fit into society. I never . . . I knew that my peers respected me that was never an issue but the fact that I was elected at that time in my life it changed my entire life in terms of the outlook," Sanders said. ". . . it changed the way I looked at life, the way I looked at people. People said I had a great career, what else could I want? Then to come along after all this other stuff and to say here I'm elected to the Hall of Fame. It's humbling, I always considered myself a humbling person that was different. It changed my entire life."

His enshrinement speech—just like his career—was one for the ages.

In part:

"I am not that self proclaimed Hall of Famer who desired to be in sports. I am a guy that liked a challenge, and challenged myself with the understanding that winning is finishing. To my fellow brothers in the NFL, pre-, during, and some post-players, that I have put the nails in the house that I had the opportunity to play in, I thank you for your sacrifice. I wrote a poem in 1976 that I think is fitting for my brothers.

"I realize that I was mentally preparing for a season that my body did not want to cooperate with. The poem is called, 'The NFL: Just Passing Through.'"

> Here today, gone tomorrow. If you don't accept it, it's a life of sorrow.
>
> Trying to use our God given talent, being brave like a knight, bold and gallant.
>
> Those who can make it feel lucky indeed. It's God's own way of letting you succeed.

> Our efforts we extend in hopes to win. Some play their hearts, others just pretend.
>
> So give your all and nothing less. Today we win, tomorrow we rest.
>
> You're not just my teammate, but my very best friend.
>
> Let's play together until the end.
>
> Today we hang together, just you and me. For tomorrow is a day we may never see.

Then he wrapped up by paying a special tribute to his mother, who died when he was just two years old.

"Of all the things I've done in football, and there have been a lot, there's one thing that I really, really regretted. Many times I've seen athletes, college, professional, often look into a television and say, 'Hi, mom.' I always thought that was special and always something I'd want to do but couldn't.

"So I take this time right here, right now in Canton, Ohio, at the Pro Football Hall of Fame to say, Hi, Mom. Thank you for the ultimate sacrifice. This day belongs to you, for it was written. I want to thank you all enjoying the best day of my life and may God bless you."

A special mom, a special son.

CHAPTER 7

MATTHEW STAFFORD

Quarterback, 2009–

The Game: December 18, 2011 vs. the Oakland Raiders at O.co Coliseum

DETROIT LIONS 28, OAKLAND RAIDERS 27

When the Lions drafted Matthew Stafford as the first overall pick in 2009, they knew he had the arm strength, the football smarts, the savvy, and all the intangibles that make a good NFL quarterback.

While they may have suspected it, what they couldn't have known for sure was the young quarterback's ability to take the offense on his shoulders and march the team down field to win games in the waning minutes.

Over and over again Stafford has taken the Lions from a fourth-quarter deficit to a win. Officially, he's had 15 fourth-quarter comebacks and 17 game-winning drives in his six seasons.

Lions fans learned that with Stafford leading the offense, it's not over until it's over—even if the Lions are backed up 98 yards from the end zone with two minutes and no timeouts left.

Captain Comeback.

Matthew Stafford, the first overall draft pick in 2009, took the Lions to the playoffs in two of his first six seasons. *Photo courtesy of the Detroit Lions*

There was no greater example of Stafford's ability to come back than in 2011 at the Raiders. It's a place no opponent has ever called friendly—unless you're the sort of person who has friends who throw D-cell batteries at you.

Midway through the fourth quarter the Lions were down 27–14. Down, but not out.

Stafford calls this his most memorable game in his first six seasons with the Lions.

The Game

By Matthew Stafford

It was the linchpin game in that season to help us go to the playoffs for the first time in however long it had been. We had two 80-plus yard touchdown drives with less than five minutes to go and that was basically right after I had fumbled and Aaron Curry had scored a touchdown off that fumble. So it was just a huge negative and then we turned it into two positives, made a bunch of great plays and won the game.

I just remember that game, the next week on the Saturday we played San Diego at home. We carried the momentum into that game and blew [the Chargers] out and got into the playoffs.

I know the first drive was 80-plus, I know that. And we just kind of methodically went down there and I threw a touchdown to Titus Young in the front left corner of the end zone on like a back shoulder fade.

Before that drive the play right before this drive basically was the sack fumble and Aaron Curry scoring. I was over on the sideline as they were kicking off and Ben Graham, our punter at the time, came up to me and he was like "You're just the only one damned good enough to pull this off."

I thought, "Alright, at least this guy thinks I have a frigging chance." It was pretty funny; it made me laugh for a second.

We went out there and scored on the first drive, the defense got a stop and Shane Lechler was the punter for the Raiders and he punted it down to the one-yard line, basically the one and a half yard line with no timeouts and maybe two minutes and 14 seconds or something like that. We chipped away. Then we had a third down with under two minutes. I threw a short pass to Nate [Burleson] for a first down and then a field corner route to Calvin [Johnson]. He made an unbelievable catch on the sideline, with the defender all over him. He was kind of sliding, it was a reviewed play.

We used the review as basically a free timeout. We went over to the sideline. The whole game Tyvon Branch, their safety, had been recognizing the play, jumping these basic dig routes from Calvin, and kept jumping them.

So [Offensive Coordinator] Scott [Linehan] and I decided to develop up a little play. We drew up a protection and gave them the same look, and Calvin ran the pump off of that and went down the middle of the field. I kind of had some people right in front of me. I kind of threw a high one to let him go get it. It ended up being Calvin on Rolando McClain, oddly enough [a middle linebacker], down the middle of the field. Calvin made the catch (for a 48-yard gain).

We got down into the red zone on a pass interference call. We called a play with nobody in the backfield, an empty-backfield play. Before the snap it was not a good look for the play we had called so I had a feeling I might have to run or do something. We were probably on the 6 or 7 yard line and I caught the snap and decided to take off, had Rolando McClain to beat, gave him a move and got the first down on fourth-and-3. And then maybe two plays later I threw a little inside seam route to Calvin to the back of the end zone. He made a great catch and he pretty much sealed it.

There was no question about momentum. I remember that plane ride back being one of the best. We lose that game, we

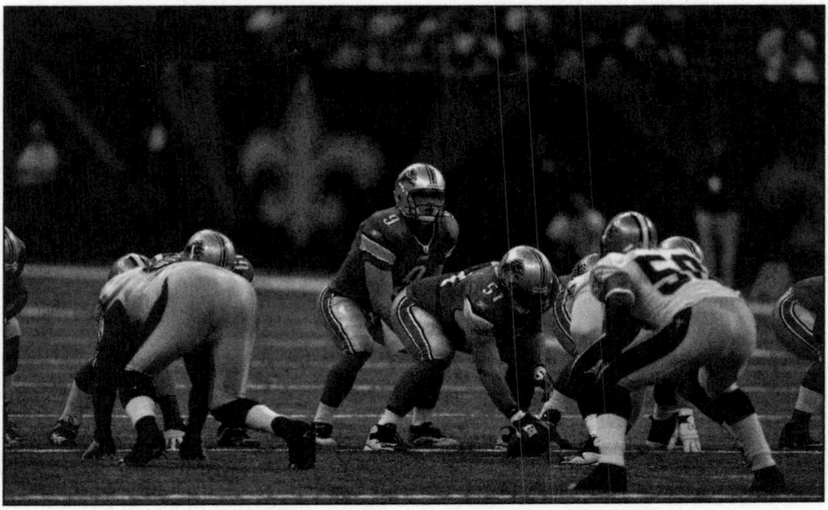

Matthew Stafford has had 15 fourth-quarter comebacks and 17 game-winning drives in his six seasons. *Photo courtesy of the Detroit Lions*

have to have a lot of help to get into the playoffs. That was the one that kind of kept us right where we wanted to be and have a chance to you know clinch it ourselves. It was just a great plane ride and obviously a long one. Guys were obviously all fired up and excited.

The next game was a quick turnaround—it was a Saturday game. We used that to kind of propel us, we came out in that San Diego game and really got after them. That was a good one.

Oakland was special too just because of where you're playing at. That's a tough place to go on the road and win.

Other Memorable Moments

Obviously, the win over the Raiders was huge, especially because of its consequences and the fact that it was on the road in a hostile environment. Of Stafford's fifteen fourth-quarter comebacks, seven have been on the road.

They're all full of drama, but some more so than others.

His first comeback was *the* highlight of Stafford's 2009 rookie season when the Lions, coming off an 0–16 season, finished 2–14.

It was November 22, 2009, at Ford Field against the Cleveland Browns who jumped out to a 24–3 lead in the first quarter.

Stafford threw five touchdowns that day, but none more dramatic than the final one.

The Lions were down 37–31 with 1:46 remaining and the ball at their own 12-yard line. Oh, and zero timeouts.

Stafford had to spike the ball three times in the final drive.

Then with 8 seconds remaining at Cleveland's 32, Stafford's deep pass intended for Calvin Johnson was intercepted by Brodney Pool. But a defensive pass interference penalty was called on Hank Poteat, giving the Lions the ball at the 1-yard line with no time left since a game cannot end on a penalty.

After that interception, Stafford was laying flat on his back just inside the sideline near the 40-yard mark. Four team doctors, on bended knee, surrounded the future of the Lions franchise.

He had been smacked but good by 305-pound defensive lineman C.J. Mosley and his left shoulder had taken the brunt of the hit.

With Stafford down, Daunte Culpepper ran onto the field for the last play.

Then Stafford heard the magic word.

"I heard 'timeout' over the loudspeaker and knew that was probably my only chance to get back in," the right-handed Stafford said after the game. "It was my left shoulder and you don't really need it to throw, so I said, 'Help me up' and they weren't going to help me up. Then I really told them to help me up and they helped me up and I ran out there."

In immense pain, he threw a one-yard touchdown pass to Brandon Pettigrew to tie the game and then Jason Hanson kicked the extra point. It was a play that Stafford and Pettigrew had worked on every day in practice that week.

"[Stafford] made a great play to finish the game, but probably his best play was eluding four team doctors on the sideline," coach Jim Schwartz told reporters afterward.

The coach asked the doctors what was wrong with Stafford and they replied they didn't know.

"Matt, he made a nice scramble on the previous play, but it's a good thing our team doctors didn't play on the varsity, because Matt had to work his way on the field. He just said, 'I'm ready.' He could walk and he was ready," Schwartz said.

On that interception, Stafford said Johnson was the only guy he saw in the back of the end zone and "he looked like he was tired as hell." He was running to Stafford's left.

"I threw it up and then got planted, and was content to lay there for a while. Then Dom [Raiola] grabbed me, and told me we had pass interference, and I was like 'Really? Come on,'" Stafford said after the game.

Stafford's five touchdowns that day were the most for a rookie in an NFL game since 1937. It was the first time in Lions' history a quarterback had thrown for 422 yards in a win. Scott Mitchell had set the old record with 410 in a win in 1995.

It was just the start of the legend of the Comeback Kid.

In his second season in Week 8 Stafford, with help from the defense, pulled out a 37–25 win against the Washington Redskins.

With four minutes and 23 seconds remaining the Lions were down 25–20 at Ford Field.

"I felt like I started a little slow, I kind of expected a little bit, you don't hope that happens but if it does you understand it. They've got a good defense, they have a lot of good players," Stafford told reporters that day. ". . . It was good to come in at halftime, get some of the feel of what they were trying to do to us and go back out there and attack it."

And so they did in the nick of time.

It was Stafford's first start since he separated his throwing shoulder in the opener at Chicago on September 12.

Stafford and the offense got major help from the defense.

Late in the fourth, cornerback Alphonso Smith intercepted Donovan McNabb to give the offense the ball at Washington's 37-yard line with 4:32 left.

Stafford capped the short drive with a 10-yard touchdown pass to Calvin Johnson, his third touchdown reception of the afternoon.

"He's Calvin. So they're playing an inside leverage on him with a guy over the top, he's got an option slant, he can take it high or he can cross his face. We were on the same page the whole day . . . which was fun. I tried to throw it at him and give him a chance, he made a great play," Stafford told reporters after the game. "He played unbelievable today, he deserves a lot of credit, so does the O-line."

So does the Comeback Kid.

That touchdown gave the Lions a 28–25 lead with three minutes and six seconds left.

The Redskins lost the ball when Cliff Avril sacked McNabb for an eight-yard loss on a fourth-and-10 play. The Lions got the ball back and in position for Hanson to kick a 32-yard field goal.

The Redskins mysteriously inserted quarterback Rex Grossman who was sacked by Kyle Vanden Bosch on his first snap. The ball was recovered by Ndamukong Suh and returned 17 yards for a touchdown.

It wasn't all Stafford that day, but they couldn't have won without him.

That Halloween win was just the second of the 2010 season.

In 2011, Stafford had three fourth-quarter comebacks including his memorable game. They were all on the road. That season, Stafford became the fourth NFL quarterback ever to reach 5,000 passing yards in a single season (5,038, to be precise).

In 2013, another comeback was dramatic in quite another fashion.

In the October 27 game against the Dallas Cowboys (Stafford's favorite team as a kid growing up in Dallas), he threw for 488 yards. But it was his sneak that was key.

The Cowboys took a 30–24 lead on a 44-yard field goal with 1:02 left. Then the Lions had the ball at their own 20 with no timeouts left.

Key to the successful drive was a 40-yard pass down the sideline to Kris Durham, Stafford's college teammate at Georgia. That got the Lions to the Dallas 23-yard-line. On the next play Stafford hit Johnson for 22 yards; he was so close to the end zone some of the Lions on the field thought he had scored. Stafford had to hurry them back to the line of scrimmage inside the 1-yard line.

Fourteen seconds remained and it was first-and-goal. Everyone at Ford Field expected a spike, including the center Dominic Raiola.

"It's just in my head, I told everybody I was spiking it, I was screaming clock, I was going to spike it," Stafford said after the game. "Kind of reading, it was a feel thing. I was yelling spike, they knew I was yelling spike. I saw linebackers standing like this [standing up]. Our guys didn't fire up, they just stood up. I looked down we were that far [six inches]. Shoot, I figure I'll get that. I was just making a play, trying to help my team win. Sure am glad I got across."

He went up and over on his first try and it might have counted as a touchdown, but just to make sure when he got back on his feet he walked it back in.

"I probably could have made it less interesting and just kind of moseyed in around the corner," Stafford told reporters. "I thought

I got in the first time. I saw how far it was and it was nothing. I felt like I used my supreme vertical and got up and got it in."

Everyone was fooled including the Cowboys defense and Raiola.

"I don't know, I squatted and tried to protect him, I saw people scrambling and he ran out," Raiola told reporters. "That [expletive] was awesome. What can you say? I had no idea still even when he scored. Right now I have no idea, it was unreal."

Stafford threw for 488 yards that day. Calvin Johnson had 329 of them, second most in NFL history for one game.

But Stafford's one-yard keeper was the key to the win.

In the 2014 season when the Lions finished 11–5 and returned to the playoffs for the second time in four seasons, Stafford had five fourth quarter comebacks including a key win at Chicago in Week 15.

One of the most challenging was a 22–21 win over the Atlanta Falcons at Wembley Stadium in London.

The offense was playing without four injured players—Calvin Johnson, running back Reggie Bush, tight end Brandon Pettigrew, and right tackle LaAdrian Waddle. The Lions were down 21–0 at the half. All along the Lions had referred to the international jaunt as a business trip. They definitely weren't closing the deal in the first half.

Then in the third quarter Stafford connected with Golden Tate on a 59-yard touchdown catch.

With 11:25 left in the fourth quarter and the Lions down, 21–13, Joique Bell had four carries for 12 yards and two catches for 22, setting up the 5-yard touchdown pass to Theo Riddick. A two-point attempt failed.

The Lions defense held and on the Lions' final possession, Stafford got the ball close enough for a 43-yard field goal attempt by Matt Prater. Prater missed, the Lions were called for a delay of game penalty and Prater nailed the second one from 48 yards giving the Lions a 22–21 win.

It wasn't Stafford's best game (24–47, 325 yards, two touchdowns and one interception) but he was just good enough.

The 2014 season was a time of adjustment for Stafford, who learned a new offense under coach Jim Caldwell and offensive coordinator Joe Lombardi.

The Lions lost their playoff game in controversial fashion on a confusing move by the officials, who threw a penalty flag for pass interference and then picked it back up.

In the first half the Lions took a 14–0 lead. Stafford had the offense rolling.

He knew he had to play mistake-free. His only interception came on a ball that was tipped up and caught by a defenseman. He completed 28 of 42 passes for 323 yards and a 51-yard touchdown play to Golden Tate. He was sacked three times.

"Proud of the guys we fought our tails off all year, won a bunch of games along the way, just didn't have enough in the tank to get it done," Stafford said.

And then it was on to the offseason.

The Aftermath

The Lions have come a long way since Stafford was drafted with the first overall pick in 2009 out of Georgia. They were coming off the NFL's only 0–16 season.

In training camp Stafford "officially" won the battle for the starting job over Daunte Culpepper.

Then his rookie season started with two losses.

"He's got it together. He's a prideful guy. He's disappointed and is not playing as well as he can and is going to through most of his career," offensive coordinator Scott Linehan said at the time. "It's our job as coaches to keep him focused on that daily improvement, weekly improvement."

Stafford threw five interceptions and one touchdown pass in his first two games. Two of the interceptions came late in the games, when the Lions were down by at least a pair of touchdowns. He was trying to make something, anything, happen. Had he not made those long-range attempts, there wasn't a chance the Lions would have scored on those possessions. As it was, they didn't score either. But he gave it a shot.

If Stafford had played it nice and safe, keeping all his passes to 5 or 10 yards, his chances of throwing interceptions would have decreased, but his chance of winning would go along with it. He was a gunslinger from Day One.

Stafford and the Lions rebounded for his first NFL win in Week 3. He was 21 of 36 for 241 yards, one touchdown, and zero interceptions in the win over the Washington Redskins.

His first two seasons were marred by knee and shoulder injuries. Because of the injuries, he was subjected to abuse from fans and even from teammate Zach Follett who called him a "china doll."

No one else agreed with Follett's claims. Stafford always has the backs of his teammates. Even as a twenty-one-year-old rookie he showed his leadership qualities. He's been respected for his hard work and football IQ since he first arrived in Detroit.

Offensive coordinator Joe Lombardi, who had worked with Drew Brees in New Orleans, repeatedly mentioned Stafford's intelligence when he first started to work with him prior to the 2014 season.

Stafford is all about wins, he has made that clear through the years. But, at the same time, he's set many franchise records along the way. Among those Lions records (all through the 2014 season):

- The most career passing yards with 21,714 breaking Bobby Layne's record of 15,710.

- The most passing yards in a season. He has the top three spots with 5,038 yards in 2011, 4,967 in 2012 and 4,650 in 2013. Scott Mitchell is fourth with 4,338 in 1995.
- Most passing yards in a game with top three spots—520, 488 and 423.
- Most touchdown passes in a career with 131, topping Layne at 118.
- Most touchdown passes in a season with 41 in 2011. Mitchell is second with 32 in 1995.
- Most touchdown passes in a game—he has 5 three times and is tied with Gary Danielson.
- Most pass completions in a career with 1,848.
- Most pass completions in a season with 435 in 2012; he's also in second with 421 in 2011.
- Most pass completions in a game at 37.
- Highest career passing rating with 83.6.

It's tough to bring a franchise back from the ashes, but Stafford has done his part in his first six seasons.

After the 2014 season, Stafford had two big milestones in his life.

One, he married his longtime girlfriend Kelly Hall.

Two, he started his foundation and announced a $1 million donation over the next ten years to reclaim the abandoned Lipke Recreation Center in Detroit.

"I have done quite a few things under the radar, kind of behind the scenes throughout the city of Detroit throughout my time here, but it just seemed like the right opportunity," Stafford said in an interview on WJR-AM.

For the young quarterback, it's not just writing a check and walking away. He plans on being a regular at the center to interact with the kids, have a little fun and be a good role model.

"This is a ten-year commitment from me and hopefully longer than that," Stafford said at a press conference.

He plans to make visits and bring along some of his teammates to the center once it opens in September 2015.

Stafford is working on the project with the city of Detroit and S.A.Y. Detroit, whose founder is *Detroit Free Press* columnist Mitch Albom.

The S.A.Y. Detroit Play Center will feature a refurbished gym along with outdoor football, baseball and soccer fields along with a 2,500-square-foot digital learning center.

Students ages eight to eighteen must maintain a certain grade point average and school attendance or enroll in the daily tutoring program to play football, basketball, and other sports at the facility.

"It's also [a way] to give back to the kids, the next generation here, the people who are going to be living here as adults," Stafford said on WJR. "If we can give them a place to go after school, to learn and have athletic stuff available to them and after-school activities available to them, if we can be a part of that and help the next generation, I'm all for it."

Stafford said the project was a good fit for his charitable efforts.

"This is a tremendous opportunity to impact our city's young people, and make a change for the better in their educational experience, best preparing them for college, jobs, and whatever else lies ahead in their future," Stafford said.

It's clear his future is in Detroit. He's signed through the 2017 season. His first touchdown pass was caught by Calvin Johnson. It's been a good connection ever since. Stafford has brought the Lions back to the playoffs twice.

The Lions have not wavered since the day they drafted Stafford. They're betting that he's the quarterback who can help make the Lions an elite team.

Chapter 8

SCOTT MITCHELL

Quarterback, 1994–1998

The Game: September 25, 1995 vs. the San Francisco 49ers at the Pontiac Silverdome

DETROIT LIONS 27, SAN FRANCISCO 49ERS 24

Scott Mitchell's career as a starting quarterback in the NFL came to an unceremonious end when he was benched after two games at the start of the Detroit Lions' 1998 season.

"What maybe people didn't realize about me is when I was there I was really competitive," Mitchell said. "The fact we didn't win a Super Bowl and playoff games ate me up. I took [the benching] very personal. And the fact that I was benched and basically left behind nearly killed me. It's such a hard thing to deal with. I believed I was part of the solution and to have that taken away from me before I had a chance to finish what I started, that was really hard for me. I couldn't let it go. I had nights where I literally just didn't sleep."

The sleepless nights lasted for years.

At the time of his benching, Mitchell was the veteran quarterback who had been the Lions' starter for the previous four seasons, taking them to the playoffs three times in that stretch. The Lions had lost both of the first two games in 1998 so coach Bobby Ross decided to go with the backup. Mitchell, who had played in 88 NFL games, was replaced by Charlie Batch, a rookie with zero NFL experience.

In fact, Mitchell has been dealing with those demons for all these years.

He only found a sense of peace after competing on the reality TV show *The Biggest Loser* in the summer and fall of 2014. He lost 120 pounds and found himself.

First, he had to come to grips with what was haunting him.

"Oh, yeah. If you can imagine being able to do what you love and then have it taken away from you and there's no going back. Your career is over, it's done. To have to live with that was such a hard thing for me," Mitchell said.

"I didn't mind the booing and the criticism and all of that. I was like, 'Hey let me play, I'll eventually prove you all wrong.' To have it taken away before you get that chance, because that's the belief I have in myself and that's what I know I'm capable of. I just didn't feel like I was able to finish that. That was a really hard thing for me and that's part of what happened to me on the show—it's what I figured out.

"I woke up every morning and I hiked around the [*Biggest Loser*] ranch where we were. I'd get up early before anyone got up at 6 o'clock in the morning, it was wonderful. I had time to think about my thoughts, you know my life and all these things that happened," Mitchell said.

"I had a day where I just broke down and started to sob uncontrollably. I sat down on the ground [and thought about] all these things in my life, all the disappointments. I gained weight, it's my personal life. I was so tired of feeling this hurt, I was so tired of feeling these huge disappointments in my life. I said, 'I'm done with this, I want to quit. I'm going to pack my bags, I'm going to leave. I don't want to continue going through this.'

"There was a voice in my head after a period of time that said if you quit you'll live with this forever. This won't go away. You just need to find a way to get up and keep moving today. So I did.

"So the next morning I was lying in my bed getting ready to get up and go hiking. This thought came into my mind that all of these things that you've gone through, all the disappointment, all the struggle—that's what's made you you. There's a lot more to you than you're giving yourself credit for and you have a greater capacity to be patient to be forgiving.

"You have a greater capacity to love and understand because of all you've gone through and quite frankly, the joy in your life comes from all the sorrow you've been through. You can't understand it without going through this sorrow.

"There was like a bolt of lightning. What I missed, this was an emotional thing, what I missed is there was all this amazing joy around me every single day and I was missing it, I was missing out on it. There was a lot of really simple things I hadn't paid attention to because I was so focused on being hurt," Mitchell said.

"Then I started to look and find some of the joy in my life. It's in food—making healthy food taste great. It's an absolute joy to me. Watching the sun come up—I go on and on. All these things it's just like, wow, if you open yourself up emotionally to joy and feeling what an amazing world we live in and what an amazing life I have. That was my journey."

He still can't believe he had a breakthrough because of a reality TV show. He's 6-foot-6 and his playing weight with the Lions was 240. He had since ballooned to 366 pounds.

"*Biggest Loser* is something I didn't want to do, I accidentally found it and I turned it down originally. Then I thought, 'No I don't want to do this.'

"I know the ridicule I'm going to get from people and they're going to say, 'How could you let yourself go like this?' Believe

Scott Mitchell's benching after two games in the 1998 season had a profound effect on his life. *Photo courtesy of the Detroit Lions*

me, I've been scrutinized before and I know hard that is. I just emotionally wasn't up for it," Mitchell said.

"What happened my dad passed away a year ago from being overweight. I watched him die over the past six years. I saw that was my future, that's what was going to happen to me, that's right where I was headed," Mitchell said. "I didn't want to have that future. Literally this show changed my life, that's how it's changed me. I never felt like I was on a reality TV show, I felt like I was having a life-changing, life-saving experience. It was beautiful, it was incredible what happened."

He was on the *Biggest Loser* campus for 114 days and lost 120 pounds.

Like the other contestants, he learned how to enjoy healthy food and also how to cook it.

"It's crazy because, well the first thing I did, I got off the airplane and went right to the grocery store and I just said, 'Here's how we're going to eat, this is what we're going to do.' I literally just dumped it in my fridge and pantry," Mitchell said. "I cook all of the meals, I learned how to cook amazing food that's healthy for you. That was a big transformation for me: to figure out how to do that. It's really fun."

His wife Wendy and his children are happy with the changes.

"Oh my goodness they love it, they absolutely love it. It's fun, there's a lot of joy in cooking for other people and having them actually like that and me as well," Mitchell said. "On top of it, it's actually good for you. Then exercise. A couple of weeks ago I had to get my brakes fixed on my vehicle and dropped it off, it's seven miles from my house and I ran back home. I just did it because I could. I live in Utah, there's an 11,000 foot mountain in my front yard. I go to the top of the mountain all the time.

"Aside from the physical side, it's more been an emotional journey which is really weird. Physically eating and exercising and all of that, I've been able to do," Mitchell said. "But it's really been more emotional. And a lot of that was from my time in professional football and in Detroit."

The Game

By Scott Mitchell

After beating the Dallas Cowboys in overtime on *Monday Night Football* in 1994, the next year again we played on *Monday Night Football.* The 49ers were 3–0 and they had just won the Super Bowl.

Ironically, the year before that we had played them, they credit the game they played against the Detroit Lions as the turning point in their season. I think they were down 21–7 at halftime and they came back and beat us 28–21. That was the turning point in their season and they won the Super Bowl.

So the next year they were coming to Detroit, they had won the Super Bowl and they were 3–0 and we were 0–3.

It was a Monday night game, everyone was like, "The Lions are going to go to 0–4 and it's going to get ugly." That was a turning point for us.

Coach [Wayne] Fontes had a players' committee and he'd meet with the players periodically and talk about what was going on. And we had this meeting and everyone said, "The problem is you've got this quarterback here and you're not letting him be the quarterback. You've either got to put the ball in his hands or not."

We scrapped our entire offense. At the time Tom Moore was our offensive coordinator.

Essentially, this was the beginning of Tom [Moore's career, who eventually won three Super Bowls—in 2006 as offensive coordinator of the Indianapolis Colts and in 1978 and 1979 as the Steelers' receivers coach]. You ask Herman Moore, you ask anyone around. We literally had five to eight passing plays that season. I threw for over 4,000 yards and 30-something touchdowns, both Herman and Brett [Perriman] had over 100 receptions, and Barry [Sanders] rushed for 1,500 yards. We literally were the greatest show on turf. That was '95 and that literally happened that week.

Playing the San Francisco 49ers we went in and scrapped everything we did and it changed everything. The offense that Tom Moore developed, that's where it started. A lot of the plays had originated when I was in Miami [with the Dolphins before signing with Detroit].

I said, "Here are some things that are really good."

They're still really good plays and I watched Peyton Manning with the Colts and I know a lot of what they were doing. I'm sure it evolved over time, but probably not a whole lot. We just simplified everything. We just let players play. We would go into games with supreme confidence. We were like "We're going to kill you."

It all started right there. We beat a very, very good San Francisco team on that Monday night.

We were behind by one [17–16] to start the fourth quarter. Then I hit Herman for a 20-yard touchdown and Brett [Perriman] to add two. [The Lions led 24–17.] The 49ers scored on a pass from Steve Young to tie it. Then Jason Hanson nailed a [32-yard] field goal for the win with a minute left. [Barry Sanders was held to 24 yards while Mitchell was 28-of-42 for 291 yards and a touchdown.]

That was quite a thrilling moment.

The season turned around in that game against San Francisco. We ended up beating them.

We went on to be one of one or two teams that started the season 0–3 and made the playoffs. [The Lions won the final seven games and finished 10–6.]

And what sticks out in my mind, Yancy Thigpen. He played for the Pittsburgh Steelers, he was a wide receiver. They played in Green Bay. If they beat Green Bay, we win the division. Neil O'Donnell throws a touchdown pass to him, he's wide open, no one is around him and he drops the ball. They would have won the game and this was in Green Bay and Green Bay ends up winning the division by the tiebreaker. I think we both had the same record. So we ended up having to go to Philadelphia. Otherwise we would have been home, which I think would have helped us. [The Eagles defeated the Lions, 58–37.]

It's just so interesting. I think we felt as a team that year, we were going to go to the Super Bowl. Football is just a funny sport sometimes. The football just bounces funny some days. I remember going into that game feeling extremely confident about what was going to happen.

Other Memorable Moments

Mitchell has other games that stand out from his four seasons with the Lions.

"My first moment is the first play that I played in Detroit. We were playing the Atlanta Falcons. It was the regular season opener, I had just signed with the Lions. I called an audible on my first play—I threw a slant pass to Herman Moore and it went for 17 or 23 yards. I thought this was awesome—this is going to be a lot of fun," Mitchell said.

"I remember in that game where we had about two minutes and we were behind and all the fans started to leave. I'm like, 'What's wrong with all of you people? We haven't even had a chance to come back and win the game!'

"It was like my first game, they've already given up. Are you serious? So what I didn't realize is people went up the concourse level [at the old Silverdome] and then they watched [the game]. I didn't realize what was happening.

"I had a fourth down and one; they [the coaches] called a pass play. I had open ground in front of me to run for the first down, but I had Rodney Holman open so I threw a first down to keep the drive alive. We ended up going down and scored a touchdown to tie it. Then Jason Hanson kicked a field goal in overtime and we ended up winning the game [31–28].

"That was my first game. I remember being asked by the press afterwards, 'What were you thinking, you had open ground and you threw the pass?' I just remember thinking, 'Wait a minute we just won the game, that was the most important thing.' I was taken aback by that question. It's really stuck in my mind."

OK, one more.

"We played the Minnesota Vikings on Thanksgiving in a barn-burner and I think I threw for over 400 yards [410]. I had four touchdown passes and I actually had another one that would have given me a record by myself; they called a penalty and it wasn't really a penalty," Mitchell said.

The Lions won that day 44–38. Mitchell was 30-of-45 and Perriman caught a dozen passes for 153 yards and a pair of touchdowns while Moore had eight for 127 and one score.

"What's interesting about that game, [as a rule], I never read the newspaper and I never watched *SportsCenter* or the news, whether we won or lost. And the reason I didn't, I just didn't want to have that distraction. I didn't want to get too full of myself if things were good and I didn't want to be discouraged if they weren't. It helped me mentally to stay focused.

"I broke the rule. I thought, 'I'm just going to watch *SportsCenter* this one time.' Are you kidding? I had 410 yards, I threw all these touchdown passes, it's going to be a good day. It's Thanksgiving, I'm going to watch. I tune into *SportsCenter* and they lead in with the story 'The great Barry Sanders leads the Lions to victory on Thanksgiving.' I was like, 'Come on, are you kidding?' I don't think Barry rushed for a hundred yards that game. That wasn't the story. I thought, 'Nope I'm never going to watch or read the news again. That's it.'"

For Mitchell, it mostly goes back to that 1995 season when the Lions led the NFL with the best offense. Barry Sanders led the offense but it was much more than that.

"It's really about moments. It's a pass to Herman Moore. That was another thing we got a lot of ridicule—Scott doesn't really have a strong enough arm to throw the ball down the field. We were like, 'We make these throws by design, I have a receiver who's 6-foot-4, he's not the fastest guy in the world, he's not going to blow by people.' If you position the ball to him, nine out of ten times he's going to catch it.

"Herman goes, 'I would rather have the defensive back on me. Then I know where he is and I can position him like a rebound in basketball.' We were really the forerunners of the back-shoulder throw. It really originated with us in Detroit. I mean when I got down on the goal line, I'm telling you right now the first thought in my mind was, 'Where's Herman Moore?' and 'I'm going to throw the ball to him, it's almost a guaranteed touchdown,'" Mitchell said.

The quarterback and wide receiver developed a chemistry.

"It was really a cool thing. I literally knew what he was thinking. I could just look at him out there and he could look at me and we just knew. Yep, this is what we're going to do and this is what's going to happen. We did some really smart things with the back-shoulder throws. You have a double move, if you get a double move and the defensive back doesn't move and the whole idea is to get the defensive back to bite, then what do you do right. We actually had a plan for when the defensive back didn't bite and it was just really smart, sound football. We did a lot of really good things, things that were ahead of our time. A lot of it was us sharing with Tom Moore. He benefited as we benefited. It was a mutual thing kind of deal," Mitchell said.

After he left Detroit in 1998, Mitchell played for the Baltimore Ravens in 1999 and the Cincinnati Bengals in 2000 and 2001. In those three seasons he started just seven games total.

The Aftermath

He still enjoys watching the NFL—even Matthew Stafford, who has broken most of Mitchell's Lions passing records.

"Oh my goodness, I really enjoy watching Stafford and that's where I am with professional football," Mitchell said. "I like to watch good quarterbacks play, that's what I understand and that's what I can really appreciate and I know how hard that it is to do. I like watching Aaron Rodgers, I like watching Peyton Manning, I like watching Tom Brady, I like watching Drew Brees—the top guys, I enjoy that. Of course, I pull for the Lions to get it together. It seems like they're headed in the right direction," Mitchell said.

"It seems like they have more tools around Stafford than they've had in the past. It's keeping that core of people healthy, it's keeping that balance together," Mitchell said.

"If you watch a team like the Patriots in years they've been successful they had a really good running back, they had Wes Welker and they had Randy Moss. And each one of those guys in and of themselves could beat you one-on-one. If they just had Wes Welker, you could shut Wes Welker down. It's having enough firepower to where defenses can't lock into one thing," Mitchell said. "That's when they've really succeeded when they've been able to create that. I see the Lions, they had more weapons and more options this year."

He likes what he's seen from coach Jim Caldwell after one season.

"There are just some people," Mitchell said, "that understand the whole culture of winning."

Since Mitchell retired from a dozen seasons in the NFL, it's not like he was a loser in life.

He coached football at his alma mater Springville High School. He gave that up in 2012 to spend more time with the software business he owns.

"It's essentially a collection agency, but we work with businesses to improve their internal processes of managing their accounts receivable to either significantly reduce or eliminate the need to send accounts to collections," Mitchell explained. "We have a software platform that we embed right into their existing systems to more efficiently manage that process."

Since his transformation on *The Biggest Loser* other opportunities have presented themselves.

Mitchell is now looking to get into broadcasting and motivational speaking.

"I have my agent, the same agent for Michael Strahan. With the show there's been a lot of 'Scott looks really good on TV, he comes across quite well,'" Mitchell said.

He was planning on attending a broadcasting boot camp run by the NFL in the spring.

"People at NBC said we're interested in you coming," Mitchell said. "We'd like to cross-promote shows, it'd make a lot of sense for you to do broadcasting."

Since his football days as a handsome quarterback, he now has a larger audience.

"It's interesting, I have this crossover appeal," Mitchell said. "A lot of people who recognize me now are middle-aged women, which is bizarre. All of a sudden they see me in the grocery store, 'Hey you were on the *Biggest Loser*, I really enjoyed watching you.'"

Amazing how he turned his life around. He's healthy and just a few pounds over his playing weight.

He still loves football and holds no resentment toward the Lions.

Once again, life is good for Scott Mitchell. Just like it was in 1995.

Chapter 9

ROGER BROWN

Defensive tackle, 1960–1966

The Game: November 22, 1962 vs. the Green Bay Packers at Tiger Stadium

DETROIT LIONS 26, GREEN BAY PACKERS 14

Every morning when Roger Brown walks into the sports bar he owns in Portsmouth, Virginia, he walks past a life-sized statue of Bart Starr.

"I say, 'Good morning, Bart.' It's tradition," Brown said with a smile.

The two have a link that dates back to the early 1960s.

The bond now is one of respect between Brown, the former Detroit Lions defensive tackle, and Starr, the Hall of Fame quarterback who helped put the Green Bay Packers on the map.

Brown's most memorable game from his seven seasons with the Lions (1960–1966) was easy to determine. He didn't have to think about it for more than a few seconds.

It was the 1962 Thanksgiving game when he and the Lions beat up on Starr and his Packers at Tiger Stadium. It wasn't an ice bowl, it wasn't even that cold—it was 37 degrees. It was probably not one of Packers coach Vince Lombardi's greatest memories. In fact, that Packers loss prevented them from having a perfect 14–0 season.

And after that game, Lombardi refused to play the Lions again on Thanksgiving.

George Wilson had coached the Lions to a 10–3 record that season. Amazingly the Lions didn't trail by more than seven points at any point in any game that season. It was a record that stood for forty-eight years until 2010, when the Packers never lost a game by more than four points or trailed by more than seven. In that 1962 season, the Lions' three losses were by a total of eight points.

Of course, Green Bay had the last laugh that season winning the 1962 NFL Championship. The Lions, who finished second to the Packers in the NFL's Western division, won the Playoff Bowl (a bowl battle for third place) over the Pittsburgh Steelers, 17–10.

Brown didn't call his most memorable game the "Thanksgiving Day Massacre," but that's how others have referred to it through the ages.

"That game doesn't make us enemies," Brown explained.

In fact, when Brown was getting ready to open "Roger Brown's Restaurant and Sports Bar" sixteen years ago, Starr had owned part of a company that was going out of business. It had three life-size statues of sports icons Babe Ruth, Muhammad Ali, and Bart Starr.

"Starting a sports bar, I thought those would look good," Brown said. "I asked the bidder if I could buy them. They sold the other two and Bart wouldn't let anybody sell his.

"I called Bart and he said, 'It's yours.'"

Hence, the "good morning" tradition.

Of course, Starr has one honor that Brown doesn't. The quarterback is a member of the Pro Football Hall of Fame. The former defensive tackle who once tackled him seven times in one game is on the outside looking in.

Brown is a member of the College Football Hall of Fame, University of Maryland-Eastern Shore Hall of Fame along with the Hampton Roads African American Sports Hall of Fame, the

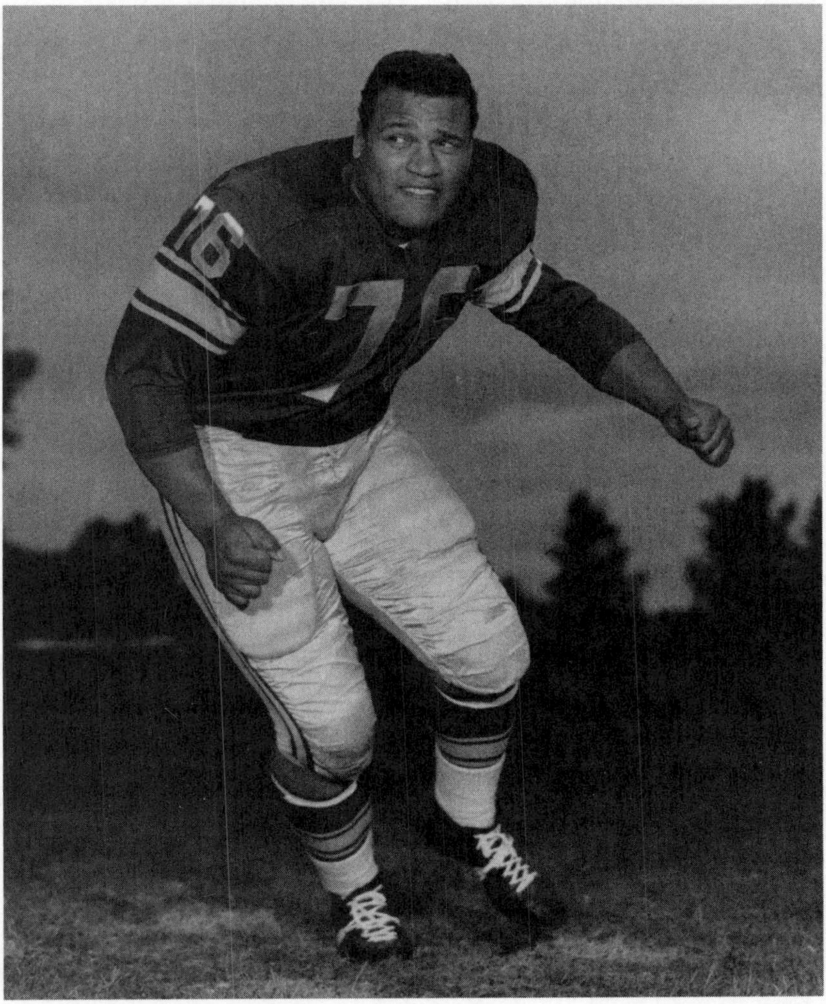

Roger Brown sacked Green Bay's Bart Starr seven times in the 1962 Thanksgiving upset win over the Packers. *Photo courtesy of the Detroit Lions*

Virginia Sports Hall of Fame, the Maryland Sports Hall of Fame and the Rockland County (New York) Sports Hall of Fame.

Just no room for him at the Pro Football Hall of Fame.

While Brown doesn't come out and say it, when you talk to him you get the sense that he still feels a little cheated. He was just a man ahead of his time.

The NFL didn't keep sacks as an official stat until 1982. Brown's record-day was twenty years too soon.

No one can take away his memories. He can recall Thanksgiving 1962 like it was yesterday.

The Game

By Roger Brown

The truth is, everybody remembers that Thanksgiving game in 1962. I think the thing that impacts that game the most is that we got beat the last couple of minutes in the [previous game against the Packers] up at Green Bay [losing 9–7] and we wanted to prove a point.

When I think about the different games I played in, I played in a lot of outstanding games—some with the Chicago Bears where I picked up Ted Karras and threw him into Bill Wade and knocked him down in the end zone.

I think a game like 1962 against Green Bay was a highlight of my life because it was something we really needed to prove. I think we all—the whole team, not one person, not one play, but the whole team—went out to show them that not so much that we were the better team, but that we just wanted to get recognition and pay them back for taking a game away from us.

Green Bay was the favorite, definitely, because they beat us in the first game in Green Bay. They were undefeated [13–0] going into that game and we had lost a couple of games [10–3].

[Lions quarterback Milt Plum didn't have a great day, throwing two touchdowns [both to wide receiver Gail Cogdill] and two interceptions. But that was two more touchdowns than the stingy Lions defense allowed quarterback Bart Starr, who was 11 of 19 for 49 net passing yards and minus-6 yards rushing on four carries.]

We were definitely fired up because it was a Thanksgiving Day game. When you think back with the Thanksgiving Day game with the Detroit Lions and the Green Bay Packers that was the only game on the television. That was national television. That wasn't a weekend game or just a makeup game. It was nationally televised so everybody while they ate their turkey leg watched that football game.

The other thing that gets me fired up constantly was in that game I tackled the quarterback Bart Starr seven times, one of them was for a safety and Sam Williams got the fumble.

The thing that bothers me was that was one game, one week, nationally televised, everybody and God saw the game, and [now] they say that this guy that plays for the Kansas City Chiefs [Derrick Thomas], set the National Football League record by having [seven] sacks in one game. Back [in 1962] they didn't keep [sack] records. That's all they tell me, well we didn't keep records.

Well, whose fault is that? I'm not saying go back and check and look at a whole 14 games that we played. Just one game, one day, one week that's all there was and it was nationally televised. I haven't got it [credit] yet. I don't think I will but I think everybody knows. Eleven sacks [in one game] and I had seven of them.

It was not my best game, but it was one of my outstanding games. I had good games against the Bears, the Rams, you name it. I did pretty good. I know in 1965 in total [I had] 19 sacks just that season because the defensive coaches used to keep track of how many times you got to the quarterback and that record I have on my performance. So I had some good games.

That day was a standout.

Other Memorable Moments

It was quite a Lions defense. Two future Hall of Famers—Dick "Night Train" Lane and Dick LeBeau—intercepted Starr that day. Yale Lary, another Hall of Famer, punted and played defensive back.

Milt Plum wasn't just the Lions' quarterback, he also kicked a 47-yard field goal that gave the Lions a 26–0 lead when the fourth quarter started.

It was an all-time thrashing, nationally televised.

That game was not Brown's only claim to fame.

In 1962, he was part of the Lions' Fearsome Foursome along with Alex Karras, Darris McCord, and Sam Williams. (The Rams' Fearsome Foursome in 1963 with Rosey Grier, Lamar Lundy, Merlin Olsen, and Deacon Jones was more well known than the Lions' defensive line with the same nickname.)

That season he was named the Outstanding Defensive Lineman in the NFL, tying an individual NFL record for safeties scored in a season (two) that had been set thirty years earlier. Brown had also sacked Johnny Unitas along with Starr. That record of two safeties in a season still stands. It's been matched by many but never beat. Also in that 1962 season, Brown had 19 sacks.

When Brown was traded to the Los Angeles Rams in 1967 he became a member of their Fearsome Foursome, which included Deacon Jones, Merlin Olsen, and Lamar Lundy. Brown replaced Rosey Grier, who retired in 1966 after a career-ending Achilles' injury.

It's not just the record books that give an indication of the type of player that Brown was. He still takes credit for inventing the "head slap" even though it was Deacon Jones who made it more famous.

"I think the Lions today have a great defensive team, I think they have a good defensive line. I think [former Lion] Ndamukong Suh is a good ball player, but he can't do the things that we used to get away with," Brown said.

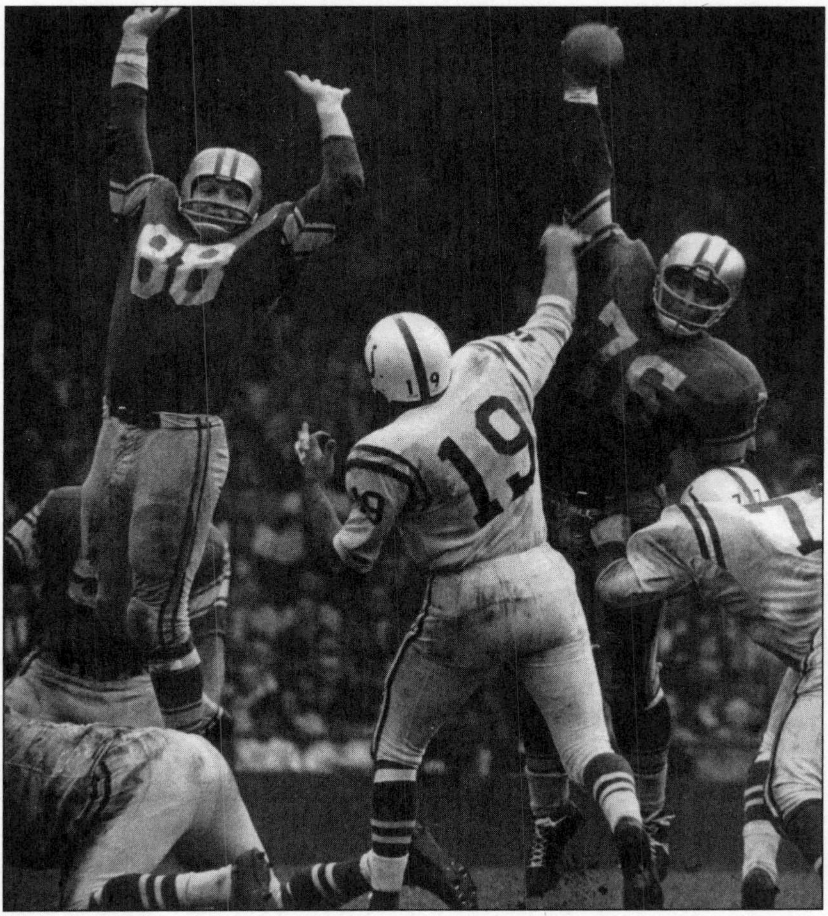

Roger Brown didn't just excel at sacks. At 6-5, he could also bat away passes—this one against Johnny Unitas. *Photo courtesy of the Detroit Lions*

"I invented and brought in the head slap that Deacon Jones wrote a book about [*Headslap*, published in 1996]. I said, 'Deacon, why are you writing like you brought the darned thing in?' He said, 'Well, I didn't invent it or start it. I just perfected it.'"

In an interview with the *Los Angeles Times* in 1999, Jones confirmed this. "The head slap was not my invention, but Rembrandt, of course, did not invent painting," he said.

And back in the day it was totally legal. Hard to imagine.

"You could hit a guy aside the head, with a fist just go aside the head and stun him," Brown said demonstrating the move with his fist. "You can't do that today. You can barely touch them."

Ed Flanagan, a four-time Pro Bowl center, played with Brown on the Lions and against him as a member of the San Diego Chargers.

"He was a bear. He made a lot of offenses, especially offensive linemen, happy when he retired," Flanagan said in a story by JW Nix at BleacherReport.com. "He was really smart, tough, and worked hard. He could read what you were going to do before you did it. He had everything. He had size, quickness, and speed, and he ran a 4.8 40-yard dash. He was the consummate All-Pro. I easily put him on the level of Hall of Famers Bob Lilly and Merlin Olsen. Roger should be in Canton himself.

"I remember joining the Lions as a rookie in 1965. He ran over me and through me all day in practice. I called my dad and told him I didn't think I was going to make the team because Roger Brown was destroying me in practice every day. His head slap could knock a head off because he was so strong," Flanagan added.

The Aftermath

Brown retired in 1969 after breaking his hand and struggling through the season. His second career was already in motion as the owner of a restaurant in Chicago. He walked away from the game he loved while still in good health. Partly it was a business decision because at the time he was making more in the restaurant business than in the NFL.

Brown was one of the first NFL players to weigh in at 300 pounds; it was his speed and size that made him the player he was.

He said he watches the Lions play on television whenever he gets a chance.

In October 2014, he made his way to Ford Field when defensive linemen from throughout the years were honored.

It's been nearly fifty years since he played. Brown, a six-time Pro Bowler, wrapped up his NFL career with the Los Angeles Rams from 1967 to 1969.

He said there is one way to compare the era he played in and the NFL today.

"You could in a way because in both eras you have to adapt quickly on the field. If one player blocks a certain way or if he's holding you, you have to adapt, you have to get around it," Brown said. "If a player is chopping your legs out you've got to fix that too. What they cannot do, they can invent something else.

"I learned a long time ago, never sit and argue with an offensive lineman. He wants to fight you on the line because he's doing his job, he's keeping you away from yours," Brown said with a chuckle.

It wasn't easy to take Brown off his game.

He was one of the best at what he did. Just ask Bart Starr.

CHAPTER 10

JASON HANSON

Kicker, 1992–2012

The Game: October 20, 2002 vs. the Chicago Bears at Ford Field

DETROIT LIONS 23, CHICAGO BEARS 20, OT

A kicker has a different view of an NFL game than the rest. For twenty-one seasons, Jason Hanson was in the midst of the action for the Lions.

He has vivid memories but they don't always coincide with Lions' victories.

Several of his banner days have gone forgotten because of a loss. Or because some other guy had a day that also was a standout.

"I remember the time we beat the Packers on Thanksgiving [in 2003]. I went five-for-five, I kicked five field goals," Hanson said. "I made three in the third quarter and really helped put the game away and put us in the lead."

The Lions beat the Packers that day 22–14 and indeed Hanson scored 15 of the Lions' 22 points on field goals of 42, 28, 49, 46, and 32 yards. He out-scored the Packers by himself.

"I was super excited. At the end of the game I was in the middle of the field when the game was over and Dre Bly was there too. The TV production people come running up and they grab Dre Bly for player of the game. I remember thinking, 'I hate being the kicker,'"

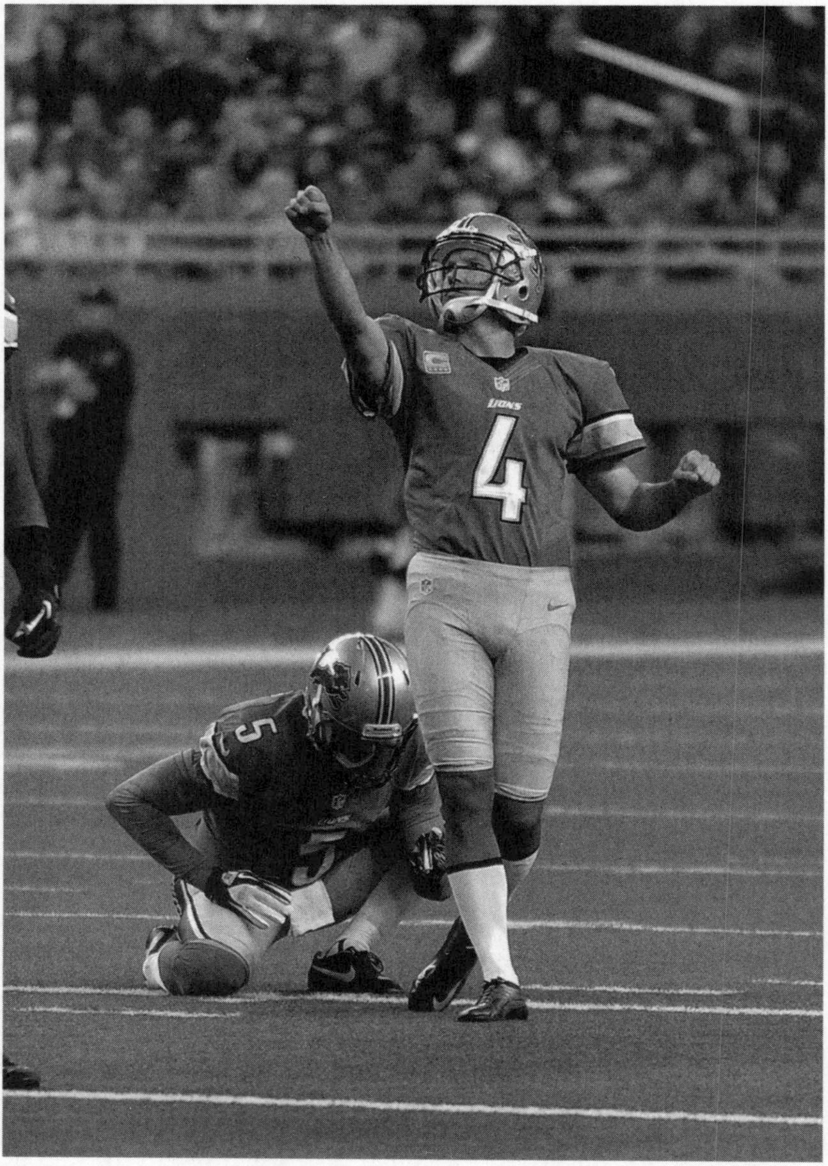

Kicker Jason Hanson was Mr. Automatic for twenty-one seasons with the Lions. *Photo courtesy of the Detroit Lions*

Hanson said. "It was like I was super excited about what I did, but it was no big deal because Dre had two interceptions."

He recalls another game, though, where he did at least get some recognition. Not as much for his kicking as his tackling prowess. It was a 31–28 overtime win over the Atlanta Falcons in the regular season opener in 1994.

"What happened in this game was I ended up kicking a field goal to win at the end of the game. I kicked the game winner. I kicked an extra point to tie the game right before the end of regulation. When we kicked off, the guy [Alton Montgomery] broke through, I tackled him and basically saved him from returning for a touchdown. So we went to overtime and I kicked the game winner," Hanson said.

He couldn't remember the exact date or even which season, but Hanson knew it was during the Chris Spielman era.

"When I get home, there's a call on my answering machine and so I walk in the door and—this is perfect Chris—I pick it up. 'Hi Hanson, this is Chris. Nice tackle, bye.'

"He didn't say a word about winning or the game-winner all he cared about was the kicker had made a tackle, all was right in the world for him," Hanson said.

Hanson also didn't remember that he was injured on that tackle. He squibbed the kick because the Lions didn't want the Falcons to have a chance to return it. But when Montgomery turned up-field, Hanson was there and the only one who could prevent a game-winning touchdown by Atlanta. Montgomery's knee came down on Hanson's shin. The Falcons tried a 52-yard field goal to win, but it was wide.

Meanwhile the trainers were working on Hanson's calf along the sideline. Reports from the game said Hanson was in obvious pain when he kicked the 37-yard winning field goal in overtime.

It wasn't just Spielman who appreciated Hanson's effort that day.

For the one game that really is most memorable, it's quite easy for Hanson to remember the exact date. There's a good reason for that.

The Game

By Jason Hanson

That season my wife was pregnant with our third child who is Luke, our son. She had some complications so she had to be on total bed rest. We spent the offseason out in Washington state. So she couldn't come back for the season because she had to be on bed rest and had to be with family to help. I was home for the season.

Because of the complications she was scheduled for a C-section on October 21 which was the day after the game. So I had the last flight out of the day out of Detroit to reach Spokane on Sunday evening. It left around 6 o'clock.

I was good; it was going to be tight. I was good as long as the game didn't extend or go into overtime. So the game goes into overtime.

We kick off, we get the ball. I think we run six plays, we get some chunk yards. So after six plays I'm trotting out on the field to kick a 48-yard field goal to win.

The life of a kicker is pressure. I make this kick, we win the game and then I run in and I most likely make the flight and I see my son be born the next day. If I miss this kick, we lose the game, I most likely miss my flight because the game is extended and I don't see my son be born. So I'm kicking a field goal to see the birth of my son. No pressure.

I make it. Then at the end of the game, I'm trying to get off the field and run in. Marty Mornhinweg's post-game speech seemed to last forever because I was trying to get in the shower and get out of there—literally.

The short story is I get to the airport and I literally get to the gate, just seconds before they're doing last call, just seconds before they're going to close the door. I make it, I'm sweating, I get on the plane.

The next morning I'm at the hospital in Washington holding my new son.

I remember that one vividly.

Other Memorable Moments

"As a kicker you have memories of things that are insignificant to the world that are huge to you—technical things," Hanson said.

He recalled a game at San Francisco in 2001 when the Lions lost 21–13.

"First half, perfect conditions and then this wind comes out of nowhere. It's like 39 mph and I can't keep the ball on the tee," Hanson said. "I miss a field goal [from 43 yards, wide right] in the first half. It's kind of a bad game and it's tight.

"We're driving and the wind is unbelievable. It's like a 45-yard field goal and coach sends me out. I remember being so angry, I'm thinking I'm about to miss another field goal.

"I kick it, it curves left, it curves right, and drops in. To that point in my life it's the greatest kick I ever made," Hanson said. "And so I'm like yelling and I'm super excited. Nobody's looking at me, nobody cares. It was a 45-yarder. You're supposed to make those. I'm standing there thinking I just had the greatest kick of my career and nobody on this field cares what I just did. They're thinking about we're losing and I missed one earlier."

It's the life of a kicker. Hanson's 21-year run with the Lions was an amazing stretch. He holds the franchise record for most points in a career with 2,152. Kicker Eddie Murray is second with 1,113.

He holds every Lions kicking record. He's tied with Garo Yepremian for six field goals in a game. He's kicked his longest field goal of 56 yards twice. Hanson also has the most field goals in a Lions career with 495 and is among the top five for most in a season, with 34 field goals in 1993.

Hanson went to the Pro Bowl in 1997 and 1999. He was first team All-Pro in 1993, 1997, and 1999. His career field goal percentage was 82.363 and best season for field goal percentage was 2003 when it was 95.652 percent. His second-best percentage for a season was in 2008, at 95.455.

"Our 0–16 season in 2008 I had my best season ever, a couple games where I kicked some field goals at the end or kicked a couple 50 yarders to keep us in it," Hanson said. "I thought we were going to go down and finish it off we never did, so they're all forgotten field goals."

Certainly it was frustrating.

"I mean, yeah, kicking is something where obviously being 0–16 and the sting of the losses everybody was in on that, the depression of playing that bad," Hanson said. "But there was something about doing your thing, so you're feeling good about what you're doing individually.

"When you're losing nobody cares. So a lot of times it was just the guys in the building who would know that you kicked some important field goals or you're kicking well, but nobody across the league was worried about it. Just a strange, sad season. I think we were 4–0 in the preseason.

"Kicking is a weird thing. You're pretty individual in what you do, but at the same time even though it's individual you're still wrapped up in what's happening with the team," Hanson said.

And some years were better than others.

The Barry Sanders era was, of course, special.

One game that stands out for many was the final regular season game at the Silverdome in 1997 when Sanders broke the 2,000-yard mark for the season and linebacker Reggie Brown crumbled to the turf with a spine injury.

"I just remember some of the Silverdome games because we had been winning and there were some big moments," Hanson said. "You get 80,000 people in there . . . some of my best home memories are in the Silverdome and that's one of them. Last game of the season, needing a win to go to the playoffs and Barry breaks 2,000 and just the surrealness of Reggie getting hurt and the way some guys were reacting. People were scared.

"I don't know if we knew at the time until afterwards that he had stopped breathing. There was a feeling that it was bad. There were these huge emotions. You have the loss of the guy getting seriously hurt and Barry Sanders getting an epic milestone, and winning. There are the ups and downs of football in a single game. Silence when Reggie is hurt and you can't hear yourself think when Barry breaks the record. It was an incredible game."

It's clear that Hanson has great memories of the Silverdome where during his years the Lions had a better winning percentage than they did when Hanson kicked at Ford Field.

"The Silverdome could be unbelievably loud. Just the amount of people [it held more fans than any other NFL stadium for many years]. The Detroit fans are great. There were big games, in that era and so when Barry broke the record—that's what the NFL can be like when the team does its part and plays well. The fans are [appreciative], it's a crazy experience—the roar of the crowd."

Even now, Hanson said he tells his children about playing with Barry Sanders. They were too young to appreciate Sanders at the time, but are able to confirm what their dad tells them via highlights on YouTube.

"It's amazing to have been teammates with one of the greatest players ever to play and who was so good you still watch his runs. I laugh when I watch them—I'm thinking I was on the sideline for that one."

Sanders is a big reason the Silverdome crowds were so loud. "Yes, it was Barry and it's also [because] we were competitive and winning and all of that together. We were working toward the playoffs. We were in the playoffs," Hanson said.

For a kicker it was a different experience never knowing exactly what Sanders would do once he had the ball in his mitts.

"You were seeing things that you didn't see anybody else do. On the field is a collection of some of the best athletes in the world. And to watch one man embarrass some of them, it really was incredible," Hanson said.

"Usually as a kicker I start to warm up when we kind of get close to mid-field. You anticipate the drive. I remember with Barry, when we got the kickoff and got on the field, I would kind of start to get ready. You didn't know what was going to happen. All of a sudden one play we're in field goal range. Or in one play I'm kicking an extra point. Twice in a game at Tampa we're at our 20 and I have to kick an extra point in one play. Twice."

Sanders had 80-yard and 82-yard touchdown runs in that one October 1997 win over the Buccaneers.

"Usually when we were at the 20 that's when the punter warms up. I'm out of his way he's in that zone when we might punt," Hanson said. "Next thing you know I'm slapping my helmet on thinking 'I didn't even warm up, you took me out of my routine.' With Barry there was always that threat."

Sanders retired before the 1999 season, so Hanson played fourteen seasons without him.

"Having some perspective again now, I played a decade or longer afterward without him, being in the league or being out. That's why he was Barry," Hanson said. "You see the film. He just did things that were so special that nobody else does. He was a great guy. It was always amazing that you played with one of the greats ever."

Hanson is in that category for Lions fans. Perhaps they didn't appreciate him enough because they were so spoiled. He was Mr. Automatic for so many years at the Silverdome and then at Ford Field.

He appreciated the fans then and still does now, in his own way.

"I always thought it was cool when they [the fans] protested and marched on Ford Field," he said laughing. "It was when we were bad, really bad—that whole Millen thing."

Indeed hours before a game in December 2005, about a thousand fans gathered and marched on the streets around Ford Field protesting the ineptitude of Lions general manager Matt Millen. They chanted "Fire Millen" and "Ho-ho-ho, Millen must go."

"It seems strange to say that, how cool is that that our fans are so passionate that they're going to protest," Hanson said.

"I've been in stadiums before. I remember one time playing in Atlanta when they weren't very good, there was just apathy. The stadium was half full and it was quiet. It was so strange. But here in Detroit, people were mad. I actually thought in a strange way that said a lot about the fans.

"There were a lot of complaints and, as a player, you'd say, 'That's off base.' But they had that right, they loved the Lions and they were sick of losing," Hanson said.

"The fans were always great. Again, I feel Seattle, of course, has the 12th Man which is a big deal in that stadium. We played out there toward the end [of my career] a couple times and it was incredibly loud. But I just know there were times in the Silverdome when again, in big games, I heard just deafening roars. I remember those being as loud as Seattle or anywhere else. The point I'm making, the fans are so passionate. I have lots of memories, especially in the 1990s when we were in some big games it was incredible—ground shaking, roaring build-up to those games and the fans were always incredible."

Of course there was a ten-year streak at Ford Field when the Lions never had a winning season. Still, the fans were there.

"I go back to the fact that losing games and the fans still showing up and watching us play was always amazing," Hanson said.

Like so many of the former Lions, playing on Thanksgiving was always special for Hanson too. It's been a tradition in Detroit since 1934.

"I think it's because it's bigger than you. It's special to the city, it has some history. That feeling, that excitement," Hanson said. "There's something as a professional football player, when you get in the stadiums, there's an atmosphere. There can be a buzz to the stadium on big game days. There's more activity, there's more noise when you're warming up. Sometimes it can be quiet and still. Sometimes a lot of us would go out on the field and loosen up before the fans saw us in our jerseys. We're out there maybe two hours before the game in sweats, starting to get loose.

"Thanksgiving is a game [when] there's more activity, there's more noise in the stadium, you can feel excitement and you can feel anticipation. Part of the buildup to the game is that you can experience it in the stadium.

"The amazing thing even in the seasons in the 2000s when we didn't have good records and we weren't super competitive . . . in those seasons up to those games, for the most part Thanksgiving had that buzz. Where maybe the game before maybe you were booed off the field. There was always something special. It was nationally televised, of course, more people floating around. Even in the years when we were bad, that game was always still good as far as the fans and that atmosphere and the excitement," Hanson said.

He said it was the same at other times of the season when they were in nationally televised games.

"As something that happened again in those years when we were bad, you didn't have many nationally televised games. If you went on the road or we finally got a *Monday Night Football* game after so many years—we had one that was a preseason game. The excitement of the fans was so unbelievable. You were kind of angry inside that this is what it should be. This is what the NFL is like, incredible atmosphere and so those national TV games when the spotlight is on. It's something that all players like. There's a different feel to those big games. I know the NFL is important, they always seem to carry a little extra. That's the fun of winning, it seems like you're always in those games in the spotlight. Thanksgiving was for sure always one of those big special games for our team."

A special road game each season was traveling to Wisconsin to play the Green Bay Packers. When Hanson first started with the Lions, the Packers would play some of their games in Milwaukee. While Hanson was with the Lions, they were never able to beat the Packers in the state of Wisconsin.

The last time that happened was in 1991, the year before Hanson was drafted in the second round out of Washington State.

"In the first year or two we played up there [in Milwaukee], I thought my career was over because the field was frozen and I couldn't keep my balance," Hanson said. "One of the things about my style is that I always was pretty aggressive on how I came into the ball. I liked to kick it hard, and so I'd come flying in and I couldn't. I was sliding, I couldn't kick the ball in the pre-game warmups.

"I thought they were going to hire somebody else next week because I'm going to miss everything I try today. Chris Jacke was the kicker for Green Bay and he saved my life. We were talking before the game. I said, 'This is ridiculous how do we do this?' He said you get the longest cleats and you kind of stomp down through it, you break through the crust and they stick," Hanson said.

"Up to that point I'd never worn replaceable studs. We were turf outdoor field in college. We played California schools and Arizona. Everybody else out there had turf. It wasn't something I had to deal with was frozen tundra. So I went in before the game and got the replacement cleats. They looked like spikes—about five-eighths inches, the longest allowed. I had to lift my foot up and stomp down, you could feel them crunch down. I might have missed one field goal that day but I made my extra points. I survived."

Even though he never won there, Lambeau was not his least favorite field. Of course, it wasn't his favorite either.

"We had a playoff game up there early in my career; it was super tore up. It wasn't frozen but it was destroyed and muddy and as a kicker I hated that," Hanson said. "Most of the time in Green Bay toward the end it was amazing—the technology they had to keep the grass green into November up there. It was amazing technology they took from European soccer.

"While there was some real cold games up [in Green Bay], I always hated Chicago's Soldier Field more. It seems like it wasn't taken care of as well. It's a municipal stadium [and] it was shared with other high schools and groups. I played a frozen game when I had to wear turf shoes in Chicago.

"I always kicked well at Green Bay for some reason, I never looked forward to going there but I always kicked well. It seems like we played there quite a bit late in the year, so finally one year we opened up there. I was ecstatic to get opening day at Green Bay. I think it was 38 and raining in September," Hanson said. "I couldn't win."

He was drafted in 1992 and starting in 1993, the Lions made trips to the playoffs in five of seven seasons (1993, 1994, 1995, 1997, and 1999).

"Yes, but they're all bad memories," Hanson said.

"We won six in a row and walking into Philadelphia and being down 51–7 in 1995, not a good memory," Hanson said.

"In 1993, we were a good team and played well; we actually had beat Green Bay at the Silverdome in the final regular season game," Hanson said. "So we didn't think there was any chance they could beat us in the first playoff game at the Silverdome a week later."

"Then of course they get close to midfield and Brett Favre throws the long touchdown to Sterling Sharpe. The incredible deflation," Hanson said.

Favre's 40-yard touchdown pass with 1:05 remaining gave the Packers the 28–24 lead that stood. The Lions got the ball back with 51 seconds remaining, but quarterback Erik Kramer couldn't make anything happen. Hanson had put the Lions on the scoreboard first in that game with a 47-yard field goal.

That was just Hanson's first playoff disappointment.

"Making the playoffs at different times, at Washington [a 27–13 loss], at Tampa [a 20–10 loss] and just falling short in that first wild card game in 1993. Some pretty good seasons and a lot of momentum and then all of a sudden this bad feeling," Hanson said.

"I've always said the worst part of sports is losing and at the end of the season only one team feels great about their season," Hanson said. "And so there's a lot of effort, a lot of good games and good seasons that kind of get lost in the wash because we lost in the first round of the playoffs each time. There's always a sense of underachieving or failing in the end."

He said the 1995 team was the most confident and seemed right on the doorstep, ready to advance in the playoffs. Scott Mitchell, the quarterback, said they felt they could win the Super Bowl that year.

"We just went on a tear at the end of the regular season. We won the last seven and eight of the last nine after starting the season 0–3," Hanson said. "We had a ton of momentum. Lomas Brown guaranteed a win. It was cold, we were just destroyed and the final score was 51–37 but it wasn't that close. At the end the offense kind of clicked in and we scored—30 in the second half and 16 in the last quarter. The Eagles had scored 31 in the second."

"That was a good team, a lot of momentum, it was a sense of incredible disappointment because everyone expected to be better than that. For whatever reason you pull off a bad half like that and your season is over."

In his twenty-one seasons with the Lions, Hanson played for six coaches—Wayne Fontes, Bobby Ross, Marty Mornhinweg, Steve Mariucci, Rod Marinelli, and Jim Schwartz.

It was always an adventure.

"Well, every time there was a coaching change there was always a sense you have to prove yourself," Hanson said. "You know that any time, for kickers, it's one of those positions that the head coach doesn't want to worry about. The coach wants to feel comfortable.

"So if your head coach is sending you out and he's surprised when you miss, you usually have a job. If he sends you out and he's glad you made it, it's not good. Each coach has to get that comfort zone," Hanson added.

New coaches don't care about a kicker's resume. They care about what he will do for them on game day.

"You have to perform and he has to know that you're the guy, he doesn't care what you did in the years past," Hanson said. "It is a good thing in a sense that's how sports are, what are you going to do for me now. So there was always this sense of 'All right here we go again.'

"A lot of times with a head coaching change, there could be a special teams coach change too. Then everything is different. You're starting over.

"That's both sides of the coin—good thing bad thing. Bad in that you're re-proving yourself and good in that you're re-proving yourself. You've got to show up and you can't take any time off. It keeps you on the edge, it might be my last season. . . . It only takes a few misses before a new coach could say, "Well he's not a good kicker for me, we're going to think about somebody else."

But with Hanson they never did.

The Aftermath

Hanson retired in April 2013. He had suffered a heel issue but a new contract was a concern also.

"It's time," Hanson said in a statement announcing his retirement. "I gave serious thought and consideration to playing in 2013. While the determination and willpower are still there, the wear and tear on my body, especially the issues I had and still have with my heel, have convinced me that it's time to retire. I have put a lot of prayer into this decision, and I believe it is the right one."

Team president Tom Lewand had known Hanson since draft day in 1992.

"Jason Hanson is the gold standard," Lewand said in 2013. "He had an exemplary, Hall-of-Fame worthy career on the field, and for those of us fortunate to know him well, he is an even better person, teammate, friend, husband and father. Our organization has been blessed to have Jason for twenty-one years."

Hanson said retirement is good. He and his family are staying in the Detroit area.

"I mainly have a chance to do some speaking. It can be anywhere from church groups to straight corporate. It can be the whole leadership kind of message. Sometimes it's just a meet-and-greet as a former Lions player," Hanson said. "I'm doing that while people still care about [me]. I'm starting to run into kids who are like 'Who are you?'"

He's not a stranger at the Lions practice facility. He said he stays in touch with everybody.

In training camp during the summer of 2014 he showed up occasionally to hang out with the young kicker Nate Freese, a seventh-round draft pick.

"The special teams coach just said whenever you want to come down and hang out we'd love to have you," Hanson said. "I'd basically go down once in a while, I know the guys, it wasn't really coaching, just to be available if Nate had any questions or needed anything. At least he knew who I was.It wasn't like training where I was grilling them. I was trying to be sensitive.The guy knows how to kick—he made it to the pros. You just give advice if you're asked. I don't know if it was technical, he needed it to help him adjust. There weren't any one-on-one sessions. I used it as excuse to meet the new coach. He didn't know who I was."

He was referring to coach Jim Caldwell, who was in his first training camp in Detroit.

"From what I've seen and heard and just tasted a small little bit when I was down there, from the guys I know, from what they said, I think, 'Oh man, I think I would have liked playing for him.' I like his demeanor, I like his style, I think the guys respect him a lot. You can see it in the results of what they did," Hanson said.

He's involved in Lions' alumni activities.

"As far as the organization, I go down for different events, go to games once in a while," Hanson said. "I try to stay in touch without being that guy who can't leave the building."

Like many of the former Lions, he has made Detroit home.

"It is for now until I figure out what to do with my life. I have a kid that goes to Hope College over in western Michigan. My other kids are plugged in here. Nobody cares who I am any more in Washington state. It's better to stick around here where a few people remember that you played. It's good for now, until some endeavor calls me away. We're plugged into life in Detroit," Hanson said.

Detroit is happy to have him stay around.

Chapter 11

BILLY SIMS

Running back, 1980–1984

The Game: September 7, 1980 vs. the Los Angeles Rams at Anaheim Stadium

DETROIT LIONS 41, LOS ANGELES RAMS 20

Detroit Lions fans first fell in love with Billy Sims on September 7, 1980.

It's possible that Sims had the greatest start to a Lions career on that day.

The Lions were coming off a 2–14 season and drafted Sims with the first overall pick.

Management watched him dazzle at the University of Oklahoma and wanted to bring that to Detroit. If ever a team needed sizzle, it was the Lions.

Oddly enough, Sims never wanted to be a professional football player. Baseball was his true love.

He didn't want to be a running back in high school in Hooks, Texas, but all of a sudden the top two running backs were injured and Sims, No. 3, was tearing it up like no other.

He committed to Baylor before visiting Oklahoma and changing his mind.

Sims won the 1978 Heisman Trophy and was the runner-up a year later.

Running back Billy Sims scored on three touchdown runs in his first game as a rookie. *Photo courtesy of the Detroit Lions*

The path Sims took to Detroit was twisted and unconventional. Lions fans loved him from the get-go.

There's a good reason for that. In his first game he blasted out of the tunnel, wearing No. 20, and proved he was right where he belonged.

The Game

By Billy Sims

No question about it, my rookie year, 1980, my first game is the most memorable. The reason why is the fact that when I got drafted I came here and it was, of course, going through certain things, coaches look at you to see what you can do and what you can't do. They weren't really sure about my pass-catching ability because at Oklahoma during that time period, we ran the ball, we ran the wishbone. I only caught two catches—one in high school and one in college [at this point in the interview he let out a huge belly laugh]. I said, "Hey I can catch—I caught both of them." (Actually he caught three passes in college.)

The funny thing about it when I got here, me coming out of the backfield catching the ball was another weapon for me. I ended up my rookie year the second leading receiver [621 receiving yards] on the team [to Freddie Scott]. Yes, I did.

My rookie year, going through the preseason and everything, I really wasn't showing much. You could hear the mumbling, "I don't know, did we draft the right guy?" That's because of the different terminology of the game, the quarterback. There was a lot going on. At the college level you don't have all that to worry about. My head was spinning a lot [another laugh] but after the preseason, my first game, "Bam" I was back to my old self. I reacted as a runner [and] had about three touchdowns and 150-something yards [he had 153]. We beat the Los Angeles Rams who had just come off a Super Bowl loss the year before against Pittsburgh out there in Anaheim, my debut.

Of course everybody was nervous, but I was so used to playing major football at a major college at Oklahoma. We played in great games, our big rival was Nebraska in those days at Oklahoma.

I had a little jitters no question about it, can't say I didn't. I usually had jitters for every game, until once you had contact [he smacks his hands together] until once you have contact then you go back to yourself as being a football player.

I don't remember my first carry exactly, but I do know it was a good one. I just know that day got off to a good start and it continued.

When I got here they were 2–14 the year before. We ended up being 9–7. We turned it around. We lost the division to Minnesota I think there was a tiebreaker. We came in second that year behind Minnesota. We started off a pretty good year my rookie year, it continued for a little while and then I got hurt.

After that first game, I knew I was becoming myself again like in college. The main thing is picking up the terminology of the game, it's a lot. They already know you can run and jump and do all of that when they draft you. The mental aspect of the game is different. Now it's probably crazier with everybody passing. Then we were a running team; with Detroit that was our greatest asset, our running game.

My rookie year was a fun year, all the years I spent here were great. I had a chance to showcase my talent on the NFL level.

In that debut game he had touchdown runs of 10 yards, one yard, and 41 yards. His first touchdown that day (in the first quarter) gave the Lions a 10–6 lead.

Sims, who claims he had caught just two passes up to that point in his whole life, had two in the game for a total of 64 yards. In other words, he matched his life-long receiving record in his first

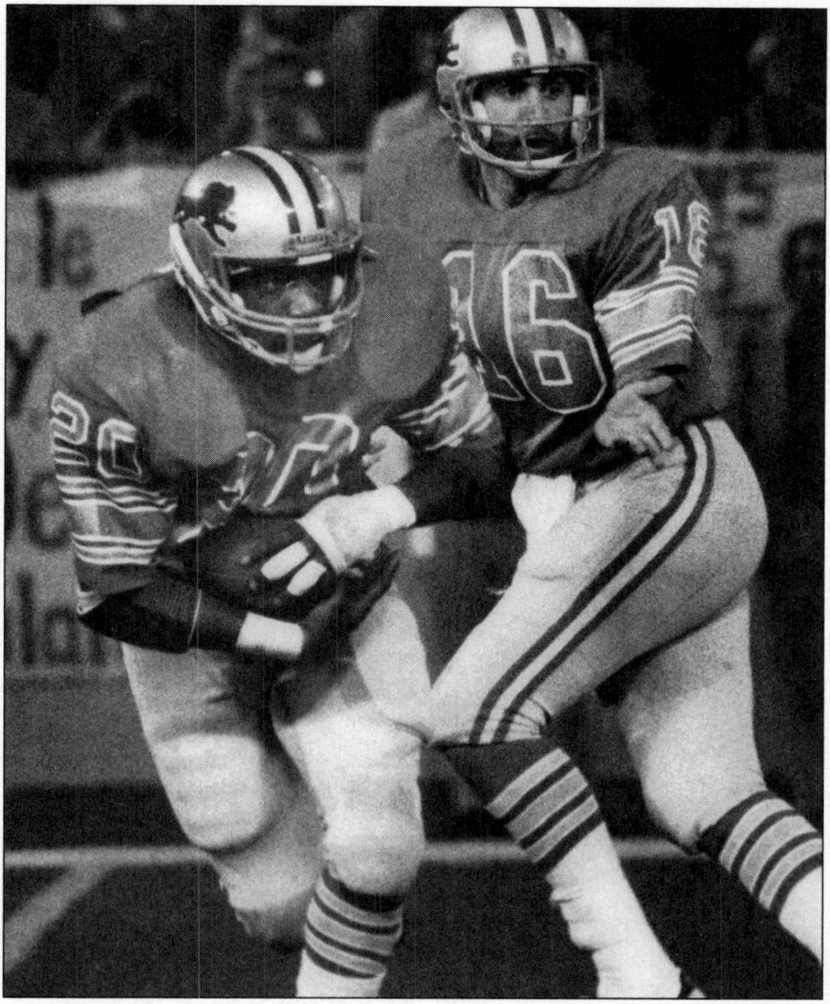

Billy Sims made a reluctant transition from linebacker to running back in high school. *Photo courtesy of the Detroit Lions*

NFL game. Gary Danielson was the quarterback. Dexter Bussey and Horace King also had touchdowns that day.

Sims was hot from the start.

His first run was off-tackle for a two-yard gain. He had eight carries in the first quarter for 40 yards. And on a pitch to the left, he outran three defenders for a rushing touchdown, per Mike O'Hara of the *Detroit News*. It was his first of 47 career touchdowns.

It was all a good sign of things to come for Sims and the Lions.

Other Memorable Moments

Looking back, many things had to happen for Sims to be drafted by the Lions.

"I wasn't like most kids, I didn't have a dream to play football. Actually I'm a big Cardinals fan. I don't say that too loud in Michigan. St. Louis Cardinals, due to the fact I was born in St. Louis and raised in Texas," Sims said.

"I didn't start playing football until the tenth grade. I was purely a baseball guy. I became a running back by default. I grew up in a little small town east of Dallas almost into the Arkansas border—Hooks, Texas, right outside of Texarkana. I played linebacker and I didn't want to play running back because the team wasn't any good and I saw the other running backs getting killed. To me that wasn't fun. So I was always third-string running back. Lo and behold, going into my tenth year when I came out as a sophomore the starting running back got hurt and his backup got hurt. I was the only one left and the rest was history after that."

Stop and let that sink in.

"If they didn't get hurt I would still be linebacker," Sims said.

He also had no intention of playing football at Oklahoma.

"About in my junior year Oklahoma started showing interest," Sims said. "Because when I came out of high school at that time, I was the second all-time leading rusher nationally in high school with over 7,000 yards [7,738 yards]—my junior year, then my senior year. I was actually going to Baylor University at that time in Waco, Texas, the Southwest Conference. Had a great coach by the name of Grant Teaff. I had already committed to go there.

"My last visit was Oklahoma. I wasn't even going up there. I wasn't going to go but my baseball coach was originally from Oklahoma. Of course, he was a big Sooner fan. I made the trip up and I had a chance to meet the great Bud Wilkinson, who had that 46–47 game winning streak before Notre Dame beat him back in the 1950s. They had a lot of great players, they had just won the national championship in 1974. I was on the 1975 championship team when I got there so they won two years in a row.

"Met the great Barry Switzer. After that everything changed. Thirty years later until this day we're still the best of friends. I make my home in Oklahoma so I see Coach all the time," Sims said. "He's fantastic—not just me. hundreds of his players just love him. He would do anything for his players even to this day.

"I can remember the biggest thing that impressed me when I went there on my recruiting trip. It wasn't necessarily about football, it was life after football," Sims said. "He instilled that in us. Coach is seventy-seven now and he still takes care of his players."

Injuries kept Sims out of the Sooners' lineup as a freshman [in 1975] and half of his sophomore season. In 1976 and 1977 he was slowed down by injuries and accumulated a total of 457 yards combined.

He was saving his best for the last two seasons with the Sooners when he was a consensus All-American each of those years.

In 1978 he had 256 carries for 1,896 yards averaging 7.4 yards per carry with 22 touchdowns. For that he won the Heisman Trophy.

The next season, his last in college, he rushed 248 times for 1,670 yards, a 6.7 yards per carry average with 23 touchdowns.

Basically, he ran his way to the top of the draft charts where the Lions were waiting.

Detroit had a decision to make. First overall picks are not always no-brainers. Billy Sims seems the obvious choice now, but back then USC running back Charles White was definitely in the mix. Sims won the Heisman in 1978 and then was runner-up to White in 1979. Sims went to Detroit with the first overall pick, while White was drafted by the Cleveland Browns with the 27th pick.

After his first pro game it became obvious the Lions had drafted the right running back.

Sims had three touchdowns, 153 rushing yards, and a pair of receptions for 64 yards.

That same day White made his debut with the Browns where he had four carries for 2 yards and 3 catches for zero gain.

So after one game, Sims was ahead by 215 yards, three touchdowns, and one victory.

No doubt owner William Clay Ford Sr. had a big smile on his face.

It was all good with the Lions for four seasons. Sims finished with 1,303 rushing yards in his rookie year along with 621 receiving yards and a total of 16 touchdowns. (See? He could catch the ball.) In his second season he had 1,437 rushing yards along with 451 receiving yards and 15 touchdowns. Sims totalled just 639 rushing and 342 receiving yards along with four touchdowns in 1982 when he was injured. Then in his fourth season he finished with 1,040 rushing and 419 receiving yards with seven touchdowns.

He was the NFL's Rookie of the Year in 1980 and played in the Pro Bowl three times (1980, 1981, and 1982).

Obviously, the fans loved him.

DetroitLions.com columnist Mike O'Hara wrote: "Sims high-stepped when he ran out of the tunnel in the pre-game introductions at the old Pontiac Silverdome. He held one arm out as though he were a plane landing as he glided into the end zone to complete a TD run."

O'Hara also recalled Sims once standing in a huddle blowing kisses to the adoring fans at the Silverdome and also running out of the tunnel side-by-side with the Lions mascot with both of them high-stepping in unison onto the field.

ESPN's Chris Berman gave him the nickname of "Kung Fu Billy Sims" after watching highlights of a game against the Houston Oilers. Instead of being tackled while running the ball, Sims ran at, jumped, and while fully airborne kicked the Oilers tackler in the head.

He loved the game and it showed. No wonder fans loved him.

Sims got off to a hot start in the first eight games of the 1984 season with 687 rushing and 239 receiving yards with five touchdowns.

That was where his career came to a screeching halt.

"It was the eighth game of the season at Minnesota," Sims said. "A few plays before that I had become the all-time leading rusher for the Lions [5,106 yards]. Before halftime I got hurt but didn't think it was serious. Then in the third quarter I got hit when my right leg planted in the turf—they had some of the worst turf outside of the Silverdome."

He had no idea he would never play football again.

"I kind of limped [and] got some help to walk off the field," Sims said. "Probably technology like it is now back then I would've probably had a chance to continue to play. Yeah."

O'Hara wrote in the *News* about the incident months later:

"Sims had carried the ball twenty times. When Gary Danielson, the since-departed quarterback, got the next call from the sidelines, Sims barked in the huddle: 'Change the bleeping play.'"

The Vikings had been unable to stop him but Sims thought it might be wise to try something else. Instead, he took the handoff as ordered, and ran around right end. He planted his right foot to cut back. Walker Lee Ashley, a reserve linebacker, lunged to make the tackle. Sims ducked. Ashley barely made contact.

Sims' right knee buckled. Tendons and cartilage were torn to shreds.

The pain was so intense that Sims let go of the ball and just grabbed his knee.

His teammate kicker Eddie Murray said it was ugly. It's like his foot was planted but his knee twisted around. Murray said it was "devastating" to see.

Sims lay on the turf for several minutes, then walked off with help dragging his right leg. He iced the knee, expecting to go back in. Two days later he underwent extensive surgery.

Dr. Robert Teitge, who performed the surgery, described the injury in the *Detroit Free Press*: "It was a lateral collateral and—LCL and posterolateral corner, lateral meniscus and fairly extensive articular fractures. That's a bearing surface; the bearing surface was somewhat shattered."

"I thought it was just a bad knee sprain. We flew back. That Monday I had surgery for about seven hours. When they told me the length of time [it took], I thought they took a coffee break or something," Sims said.

Still, he didn't think it was career-threatening.

At his press conference the day after the surgery, according to the *Detroit Free Press*, Sims said: "I'll be ready in 1985, you can count on that. I've been throwed and kicked by horses and cows and I've always come back. I'll come back from this, too."

"After that I tried to rehab in 1985 and had a setback because I was trying to get back too fast. In 1986 I ended up retiring," Sims said.

He tried for the comeback, but the injury wouldn't allow it.

In a 2003 *USA Today* story ranking the costliest knee injuries of all time, Sims was ranked sixth between No. 5 Edgerrin James and No. 7 Steve Emtman.

The Aftermath

Because football wasn't really his first love—and for another reason—it was not too tough on him to know he would never play again.

"When I got drafted I knew I didn't have long to play this game," Sims said. "I'm going to tell you why. I was older than most rookies. My first season I turned twenty-five. I went five years in college because I got hurt in college and missed a whole year. My birthday is in September. I went to school late, I couldn't go. Then I flunked kindergarten—my mother held me back [because] she didn't think I was ready for the first grade. It wasn't my doing; it was her doing."

Most rookies are twenty-two—many are younger these days. (Matthew Stafford was twenty-one in his rookie season.) Sims turned twenty-five in September of his rookie season.

"So I'm three years older, I'm thinking I'm playing baseball anyway. St. Louis Cardinals," Sims said. "That was my true love. I never thought about playing professional football. As a running back the average career is three and a half, four years so I just did make it. Four and a half years."

He still is second on the Lions' all-time rushing list with 5,106 yards, just one yard ahead of Dexter Bussey. He's well behind his buddy, Barry Sanders, who had 15,269 rushing yards.

Four and a half glorious years. It has always led to speculation of what could've been and that of course leads one to wonder if he could have run himself in the Pro Football Hall of Fame.

Years later he was inducted into the College Football Hall of Fame and the Oklahoma Hall of Fame.

Sims had wisely prepared himself for life after the NFL.

"Every offseason I was involved in business doing different things, I never let the NFL football part really consume my life," Sims said. "I liked it but I wasn't that in love with it, not like baseball. I was a left-handed pitcher and I played centerfield; that was my true love, was baseball. I thought I was going to be the next Bob Gibson at that time with the St. Louis Cardinals with Bob Gibson, Curt Flood, Lou Brock. In '68 the Tigers beat us, I remember that, I went to all the games. Of course, in St. Louis the Cardinals are still the team."

He may love the Cardinals more than the Tigers, but he is a devout fan of the Lions.

He's at every home game at Ford Field. It's part business and part pleasure.

It involves Billy Sims BBQ, the restaurant chain he and his business partner Jeff Jackson started in 2004 when they met while jointly working on marketing campaigns for major retail apparel brands. The two had a mutual love of barbecue (Jackson is from Kansas City) and found a successful recipe.

"Actually, I have a restaurant inside the stadium going on three years now," Sims said. "I go to all the home games. Two hours before kickoff I'm in front of the stadium interacting with the customers. Myself, Barry Sanders, we watch the game in the alumni suite."

Sims had some business adventures that weren't so successful early in his retirement. But this chain of restaurants has grown to nearly fifty with locations in Oklahoma, Kansas, Missouri, and Arkansas. He has five in Michigan including the one at Ford Field.

The aroma envelops patrons when they walk in the door. As you might imagine, the decor is simple—Lions and Sooners' memorabilia and blown-up photos featuring Sims.

Sims describes it as a family oriented, tailgate kind of atmosphere with "some of the tastiest brisket and ribs around."

Of course if you're a retired running back the slogans are almost too easy: "Run through your hunger," "Down, Set, Bite" and "Always a Win."

You can bring home bottles of Billy Sims BBQ and rib rub.

In March 2014, on the second anniversary of the opening of the location in Troy, Michigan, Sims hosted an autograph signing along with a special on pulled pork sandwiches.

He welcomed the early arrivals—they had been waiting in line at least an hour before opening on the blustery winter day—and seemed like the perfect host.

Many of the fans were too young to have seen him in action, but they had heard the stories about Sims and his magical runs for the Lions.

(Warning: Next two paragraphs may cause unnatural desire for barbecue.)

Here are a couple of samplings from the menu:

- "The Heisman: Choice of chopped brisket or pulled pork, piled high with slice of bologna and hot link."
- "The Triple 20: Pulled pork drizzled with Billy's Secret Sauce and topped with coleslaw and provolone cheese."

The Triple 20 is, of course, named after the triumvirate of Detroit Lions who proudly wore No. 20. Hall of Famer Lem Barney wore No. 20, then Sims, and then Hall of Famer Barry Sanders. Coach Wayne Fontes wanted Sanders to wear No. 20 in a tribute to Sims.

Prior to the Thanksgiving game in 2004, all three wearing their No. 20 jerseys took the field for a ceremony to take No. 20 out of circulation.

"I thought it was a great idea," Sanders told reporters that day. "I was glad they didn't retire it after Lem and Billy. It was probably a lot of good luck, I think. To be able to have this day with Billy and Lem is special."

Sims, Sanders, and Barney are still among the Lions' active alumni. All three keep an eye on the Lions, who made their second trip in four seasons to the playoffs in 2014.

"No question, I think they're turning the corner," Sims said. "I think they've got a good coach in Jim Caldwell.

"I told the people who knew me, 'Last year they got the coach there's going to be a different attitude on the team. They're going to make the playoffs, but after that I don't know what's going to happen,'" Sims said.

Sims went to the playoffs twice with the Lions and failed to win. His career was cut short by a catastrophic injury, but still he's the optimist.

Chapter 12

LEM BARNEY

Cornerback, 1967–1977

The Game: September 17, 1967 vs. the Green Bay Packers at Lambeau Field

DETROIT LIONS 17, GREEN BAY PACKERS 17

When Lem Barney was introduced during his enshrinement at the Pro Football Hall of Fame on August 1, 1992, he stood in front of the appreciative crowd at Canton, Ohio, and he sung his first words.

"For once in a lifetime a man knows a moment, a wonderful moment when fate takes his hand and this is my moment," Barney sang recreating the moment for this author. He didn't sound exactly like Frank Sinatra, but close enough.

"It was either make a song or I'll cry," Barney said. "So I did the singing, then the tears came down."

"Getting elected into the Hall of Fame was a joy," Barney said. "The first year I was on the ballot I didn't make it. The second year I was on the ballot again and everybody said I should have made it on the first. It wasn't anything I had to do with; it was the people who make the balloting.

"I made it the second year and made it in with one of the smallest classes to make it to the Hall of Fame," Barney said.

Hall of Fame cornerback Lem Barney was a seven-time Pro Bowler and named to the NFL's 1960s all-decade team. *Photo courtesy of the Detroit Lions*

He was introduced that day along with Al Davis, owner of the Oakland Raiders; John Mackey, tight end for the Baltimore Colts; and John Riggins, who'd played for the Washington Redskins.

"I have great memories of that moment," Barney said.

He was introduced by Jimmy David, who had been his defensive coordinator under head coach Joe Schmidt.

Barney is considered one of the Detroit Lions' all-time best defensive backs. He was a seven-time Pro Bowl selection (1967, 1968, 1969, 1972, 1973, 1975, 1976) and also a seven-time All-Pro selection. He was named to the NFL's 1960s all-decade team.

Along with his cornerback duties, he was a kick return specialist. Early on he returned kicks and punts. In his career he had a 98-yard kickoff return, a 94-yard field goal return, a 74-yard punt return, and a 71-yard interception runback. He also doubled as a punter in his rookie season and again in 1969 with 47 punts for an average of 37.4 yards per punt.

He got off to a great start.

The Game

By Lem Barney

Bart Starr was an icon to me in high school. I played quarterback at 33rd Ave High School in Gulfport, Mississippi. I went to Jackson State as a quarterback, but they had three other great quarterbacks in front of me so I ended up playing defensive back.

Bart was certainly an icon for me for high school and college because he played quarterback. I'm from Mississippi and he's from Alabama.

I enjoyed the Packers, the Packers were great; everybody across the country loved Vince Lombardi and the Packers.

Now as a Detroit Lion, my first regular season game, opening season of 1967, we go up to Green Bay to play the Packers, the defending Super Bowl champions.

The second play from scrimmage, Bart tried to throw a quick out to All-Pro Boyd Dowler and I was covering him and [Starr] saw me covering, so he tried to throw it low and away like a good fastball pitcher throws to a fastball hitter. I dove in front of him, I intercepted the ball, I did a forward shoulder roll, got up, and ran it into the end zone for 29 yards for a touchdown.

First pass of the game, second play of the game, Lions up 7–0. I'll never forget that.

We ended up tying that game 17–17 which was a moral victory for us.

The Packers were a tough opponent because they had the great head coach in Vince Lombardi. He would be one of the all-time, all-Pro Hall of Fame coaches.

Back then Minnesota was the frozen tundra, but Green Bay wasn't a summer city either.

For the rest of the afternoon I played good, made some tackles. Bart didn't throw to me the rest of the game.

I had a great season my rookie year, ended up tied with interceptions with 10 to lead the league along with Dave Whitesell, made the Pro Bowl, and kept clipping from there.

In your first game you have some trepidation. I had a great coach [in] Jimmy David who played for the Detroit Lions on the '53 and '57 championship teams. He was a cornerback also, the same position I played. I was comfortable with the coaching. The head coach was Joe Schmidt.

I had a quite a few picks in the preseason my rookie year. I had 26 interceptions as a collegiate at Jackson State and I played quarterback so that helped as well.

Bart and I have laughed about it [the interception] over the years. I talk to him three to four times a year to check on him. We had talked about it, he laughs about it, I laugh about it. It's just one of those things. I try to stay in touch with him and I do that for a lot of the ball players I played against.

Other Memorable Moments

Barney wasn't the only rookie that day in Green Bay.

"Mel Farr and I came in as rookies, we were rookies together," Barney said. "Ironically, M-e-l forward is Mel and backward it's L-e-m."

"We gave the league something in 1967 that has never occurred before and never happened since. We were offensive and defensive rookies of the year in 1967. We may be the only two guys who played in the NFL who have gold records as well," said Barney who was a second-round pick (34th overall). Farr was a first-round selection, seventh overall.

The two sang backup on Marvin Gaye's mega-hit, "What's Going On?"

Just like these days, back then entertainers wanted to be athletes and athletes wanted to entertain.

"During the years at Tiger Stadium, a lot of the Motown people were around—Berry Gordy with his Motown operation and a big entertainment place on the west side. Entertainers who loved sports used to come down to the games.

"Marvin Gaye used to come down all the time. We had a standing rule after a home game at Tiger Stadium—win, lose, or draw—we would all go to Larco's restaurant over across from the University of Detroit. They'd have the whole downstairs set aside for Lions personnel: coaches and wives and teammates and their wives and friends.

"Marvin used to come down to games, and so we'd bring him over too. Sometimes he'd sing a song for us down there. After a while Marvin had started getting serious about the game of football—he started going in Shirley Eder [a *Detroit Free Press* entertainment

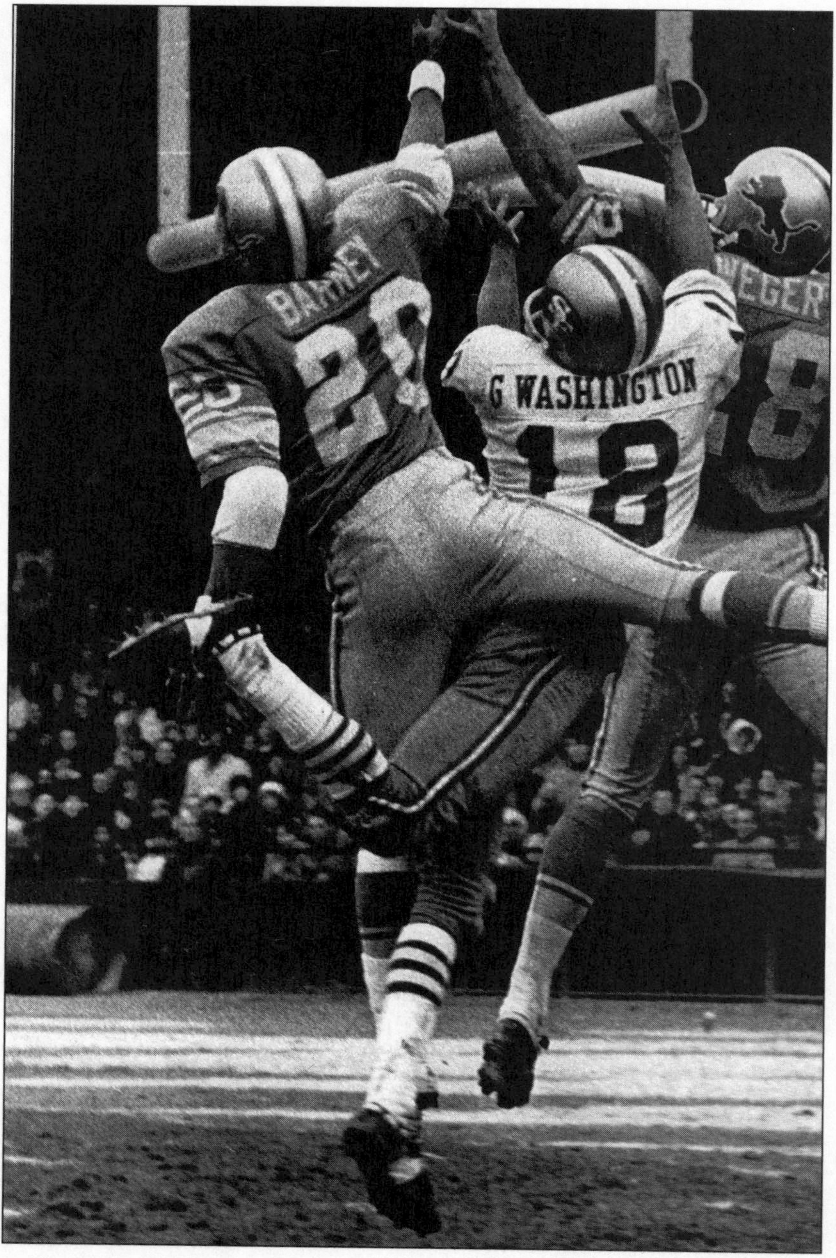

Lem Barney and Mike Weger have All-Pro 49er receiver Gene Washington wrapped up. *Photo courtesy of the Detroit Lions*

reporter] columns [and] on Johnny Carson's *Tonight Show* and say he was going to try out for the Detroit Lions.

"Coach Schmidt had asked me, 'Lem, what's Marvin saying?'

"I said, 'Coach, I tried to let him know he has to get clearance.' Everybody can't walk on. It's like if you were a mailman or deliveryman and say there's a line I'm going to go over and walk on and try to work out. You have to go through stipulations, talk to front office, management, coaches, do physicals, and different things of that nature.

"Marvin was serious about it, so he worked out with Mel and I, and we would work him. He had some good skills. The coach gave him a shot up in Flint at a two-day workout seven-on-seven.

"He had some 'want to,' he didn't have all of the know-how. He never played middle school, high school, or college ball. He just hung out with Mel and I, go out to the games with our wives at Larco's. He thought he could do it. He bowed out and gave coach a good thank you for giving him the opportunity.

"Again, he'd always say, 'Come over the studio.' We went over there one day he said, 'Lem, you take this part, Mel you take this part.' We had been listening to his music all along."

Barney had never sung professionally but he knew how to sing.

"I grew up in a church choir, church wasn't an option at my mom and dad's house," Barney said. "Then I got to college we had the chapel services on Sunday in college. Then coming to Detroit we had chapel services on days before game. I've been a minister for a number of years. I love it."

He went into the ministry about three years after his playing days were over. Ironically, the theological school was in Canton, Ohio.

Barney spent eleven years with the Lions (1967–1977). It was his only NFL team.

Barney was the first of three Lions standouts to wear the No. 20. He was followed by Billy Sims, whose career was cut short with a catastrophic knee injury, and Barry Sanders, who was inducted into the Professional Football Hall of Fame in 2004.

"I can remember all of the seasons. The one I think about from time to time, I don't know what happened. I only played in one playoff game my entire career," Barney said. "In 1970 we had a struggle. We were playing against Dallas. Quarterback Greg Landry didn't have a great game, [so] Bill Munson came in as the back-up. It was one of those things only one playoff in eleven years. I haven't done any research I think we had the lowest scoring playoff game in the history of the NFL. [Barney is correct.] The Dallas Cowboys beat us 5–0, a field goal and a safety."

Seems some things never change.

Barney said the key to his longevity in the NFL was just the basics.

"The secret was working out, training, and studying film," Barney said. "In fact, I still have an old projector from the Lions' office. I would bring film home to watch it and then have to take the film back. It's like life; you study life. It's like an education; you study your books you'll know about things on your tests. Practice was a great test before going into a game."

Barney also gives credit to his coaches.

"I had two dynamic coaches: head coach Joe Schmidt, a Hall of Famer, and [defensive coach] Jimmy David who played with Coach on the '53 and '57 championship teams and was a great instructor as well as a coach. Coach Chuck Knox, who ended up being the head coach for the Los Angeles Rams, was the offensive coordinator for the Detroit Lions for my first seven years with the Lions. It was all about studying and learning the game and executing the game and working hard in practice and studying the playbook."

Remarkably, he played across from another Hall of Fame cornerback.

"I had another great guy who was a Hall of Famer on the right side, Dick LeBeau. I played eight years with Dick," Barney said. "Then a gentleman who drafted me from Jackson State, played with Joe Schmidt, Jimmy David, and Dick LeBeau and he played the side that I came in and played in '67: the late, great Dick 'Night Train' Lane. It was a joy being a part of that Lions' organization."

Imagine the opposing offenses going against Barney and LeBeau.

"Dick ended up with 62 interceptions and I had 57. It was always a joy when Mike Lucci, our middle linebacker who was the defensive captain, would call a blitz. I can see Dick LeBeau now saying, 'Hey kid, don't let [the ball] get behind you.'"

"It was the norm for everybody like Dick and I, we would take film home after practice and bring it back the next day. It's like being a student in college: the more you study the less fearful you're going to be during the examination.

"It's the same thing, working hard in practice. This is a vow I would make. Coaches would say let them catch the ball and I'd say, 'No, coach, I'm not going to let them catch the ball. If I start letting them catch the ball in practice I will let up during the game. If you want somebody else coming out here [to] let them catch the ball I will oblige and go sit down on the bench.' They'd say, 'No, play it like you did.'"

The Aftermath

Barney, still a minister, preaches when he is called upon.

Detroiters of every age have good memories of the Hall of Famer. Either they saw him play, or maybe they just heard of his prowess. There are many who have heard him speak over the years and probably not as many who have heard him sing.

It's a long way from Gulfport, Mississippi, but Barney found a home in Detroit.

CHAPTER 13

NATE BURLESON

Wide receiver, 2010–2013

The Game: December 24, 2011 vs. the San Diego Chargers at Ford Field

DETROIT LIONS 38, SAN DIEGO CHARGERS 10

Nate Burleson doesn't go anywhere quietly.

The NFL veteran was signed as a free agent in Detroit in 2010 to be the No. 2 wide receiver. No. 1 was Calvin Johnson, the man known as "Megatron."

Burleson knew his role and would often say he was playing Robin to Johnson's Batman. He was totally good with it.

It was a great fit. Burleson had played the same role with the Minnesota Vikings when he played with Randy Moss.

Burleson brought a spark to the wide receivers group and the offense as a whole. Calvin Johnson is naturally a quiet person but Burleson seemed to open him up a bit.

His tenure with the Lions didn't get off to a great start after he sprained his ankle in the second game. He only missed two games and then came back and scored a touchdown in each of the next two contests. The first game back got him on track for his time with the Lions.

"After I came back from my ankle sprain it was the game I punted the ball into the stands. It had a few levels of why it was important to me," Burleson said. "One, I was injured so immediately I felt bad and I didn't want the city to think I was a bust or was just a guy who was going to sit on the sideline and collect a check. It was a breast cancer awareness game, we had pink on, I had pink spats on my feet."

It was a big game for Burleson and the Lions who beat the Rams 44–6.

"I caught like a dodge route, Matt [Stafford] hit me and I made a few moves and I took it up the middle and I just ran past everybody and booted the ball into the stands," Burleson said. "It was kind of like a lot of weight off my shoulders to show people what's to come and what I can do when I'm healthy here.

"But also my grandmother passed of pancreatic cancer, I was playing for so many different reasons, it was more than just a football game. That game was all inclusive. I was playing for Detroit trying to get their approval. I was playing for my grandmother because she had passed. It all came spilling out once I scored that touchdown. At that moment, I relaxed and realized I could have a profound effect here on and off the field.

"It was more of a memorable moment," Burleson said. "For me it was like a moment, with the weight lifted off my shoulders for so many different reasons."

After two good seasons, Burleson had two injuries that eventually spelled the end of his career.

In October 2012 during a Monday night game in Chicago he broke his leg and was out the rest of the season. No one worked harder to return to the field. By training camp he was back at work.

Then in September 2013, he was driving home one night when he reached for the pizza in the passenger seat to save it from sliding onto the floor and crashed into a freeway wall and was lucky to

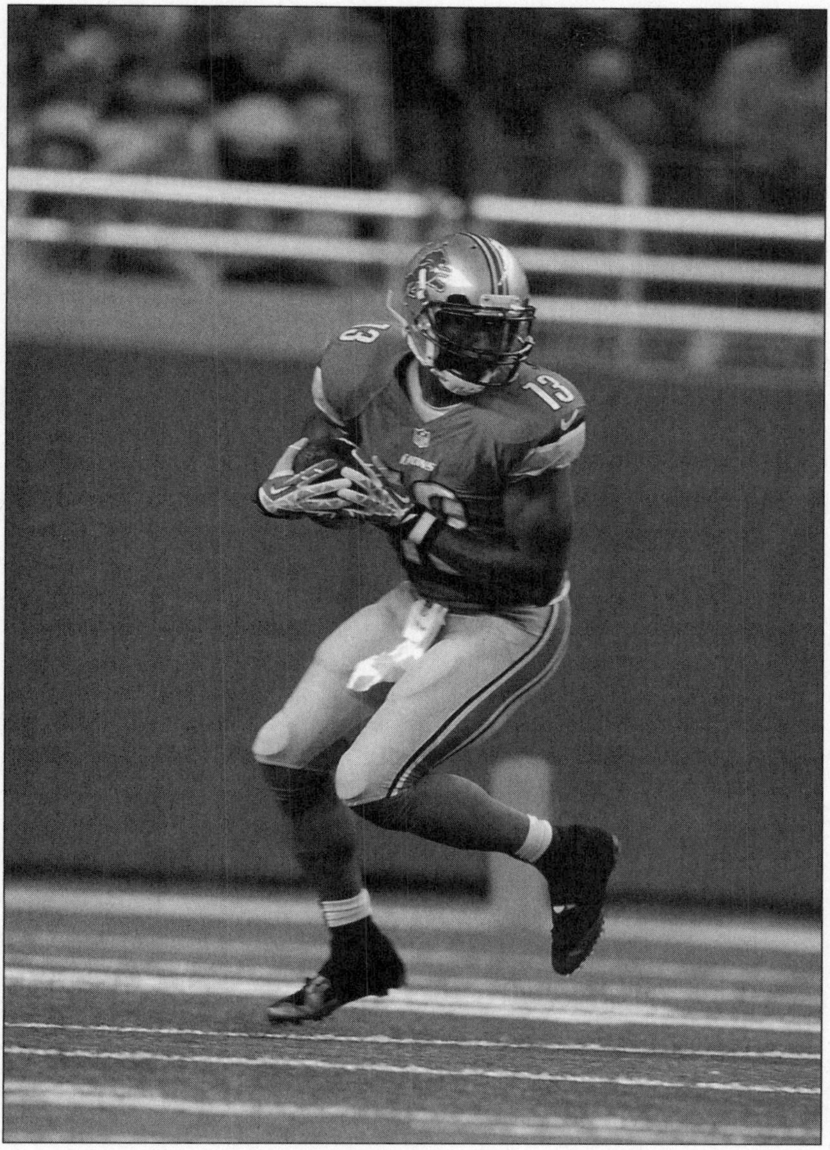

Nate Burleson knew his role as the No. 2 wide receiver. He said he was Robin to Calvin Johnson's Batman. *Photo courtesy of the Detroit Lions*

escape with just a broken forearm. He was able to return for six games late in the season.

Burleson played eleven NFL seasons with his last four in Detroit. He found a home in the Motor City. Fans loved him and it was a mutual attraction. He was perfect for the city and stayed connected through social media. He started the Lion Blood Clothing Co., that he kept going even after the Lions released him in February 2014. He went to training camp with the Cleveland Browns in 2014 but didn't make the 53-man roster.

Instead he found another home as an analyst on the NFL Network.

Here is his analysis of his most memorable game with the Lions.

The Game

By Nate Burleson

The most memorable game is the Christmas Eve game [in 2011] when we clinched the playoffs.

That was special, against San Diego. I remember being mic'd up. I was in such a good zone. I don't think I had a lot of numbers (83 yards), but I had a few catches (six). I was just open and my hands were strong.

Early in the game, it was like the first quarter, I realized we were going to win it even though it was close. I realized we wanted it more and the city needed it.

There was an energy in there that was absolutely electric. If I could bottle that moment up I would wear it as cologne. It was thrilling. It was a fun game.

Afterward no one wanted to leave. We were high-fiving the fans [around the stadium]. It was special, it was awesome.

I remember, being me, obviously a ham for the camera. In the third quarter I knew—[the Chargers] weren't necessarily packing it in but we're taking the game, it was ours. Looking at the camera saying, "It's beginning to feel a lot like Christmas." It did, it felt like I just opened the biggest gift for a city that needed something under the tree.

For that moment, it was everything it needed to be. The city was on fire, the streets were buzzing, there was snow outside, everybody was excited. You would have thought from the energy it was summertime outside. It was just so exciting to be on that field, then we get in the locker room and the music is playing, we're dancing around, we're headed to the playoffs.

Those are moments you cherish, because as you know being in Detroit, guys here in this locker room making the playoffs isn't guaranteed. I was in for eleven years and it only happened a few times.

In the first quarter you could sense it. Sometimes you walk into a game and in the first quarter you realize, "Holy smokes this is going to be a cat fight, these guys aren't giving up, we're not giving up, they're not backing down, we're not backing down. This is going to be a slugfest all the way until somebody gets knocked out." Sometimes you feel that. That's usually the games you go into it, but then there are games you walk into [and] say, "We're playing at such a high level at offense, defense, and special teams, and their energy isn't the same."

Even though the score wasn't out of hand, we just knew it. There was a certain air on our side. If you would look on our sideline, we were pressing the field, toes on the line—you've almost got to pull guys back because they wanted to get involved in the game so much. On the other side they're sitting down, they're wondering, they didn't have the same energy. That's things you can point out. I remember being on the sideline thinking, "Look at those guys, they don't want to be here." They had a chance to make the playoffs, but we wanted it more and we took it, took it early, and then we finished it out in grand fashion. That's why it was so special, we clinched with that win.

Before the game coach Jim Schwartz didn't short us on the dramatics of the game. Like he didn't hold back, he said, "Look if we win, we're in. Period. I'm not going to tell you we're going to win in two weeks. We need to win right now, it's up to you guys. Take what you want, take what you deserve, you've been working hard all year."

You know me as a vet, I was saying the same thing to these guys: "It's hard to make the playoffs. I haven't even sniffed the Super Bowl, I got close in the NFC championship once. It's hard to win; we have to take advantage of this moment. We can't wait [for] next week; next week could be gone. We could lose this week and next week is out of our control."

So we got to go out and do it. Everybody was so geeked up, so hyped, so ready so fired up, when we stepped on the field the Chargers didn't stand a chance.

[Burleson had six receptions for 83 yards, including a key third-quarter grab to set up a touchdown.]

Other Memorable Moments

All those good feelings didn't last. Burleson and the Lions wrapped up the season the next week with a 45–41 loss at Green Bay when Matthew Stafford threw for 520 yards and five touchdowns. Unfortunately for the Lions, Packers backup quarterback Matt Flynn was good for 480 yards and six touchdowns.

Then the Lions headed to their first playoff game since 1999 at New Orleans. They lost to the Saints 45–28.

"We felt like the better team but we made too many mistakes," Burleson said. "At halftime it was a close game [Detroit was up 14–10], we thought maybe we can win this. We were so young, we made too many casual mistakes that we thought we could recover from, but they were too good of a team. New Orleans was too good at that point."

The energy was so different in New Orleans compared to the win over the Chargers at Ford Field in Detroit.

"There wasn't the same approach when we got to New Orleans. We didn't have the same energy," Burleson said. "It's just different. We were on the road, playing against [Saints QB] Drew Brees. Playing at home with the crowd behind you, you're just inflated with energy and that's the tough thing about being an athlete: you have to figure out how to capture those moments when it works, capture that intensity when it's great.

"That's what makes great players great. Not to jump sports, but Michael Jordan was able to feel that way every game. That's what made him great. There were games when his opponent didn't feel like he wanted to be there," Burleson said.

"That's what makes NFL teams good. Like last year [2013] the Seattle Seahawks every day, every game was like the Super Bowl to them. . . .

"For us it was a learning lesson. You've got to be able to capture that moment and use that wherever you are—whether it's middle of the season, preseason, whether it's playoffs, whether you're home, whether you're away, whether you've got your stars playing or not, you have to approach it like that. That's how I would try to tell them, 'Hey man, let's play it like the Super Bowl. What if this was your last game?'"

The Aftermath

Burleson, who wore No. 13 for the Lions, was not an official team captain but very much a leader. He would do his best to fire up his teammates before every game. Once in October 2012 after he had suffered a broken leg and was hospitalized, he sent a video from his hospital room to fire up his teammates for their next game. It was shown at a team meeting on Saturday night and the Lions must have listened to Nate because they beat the Seahawks 28–24 the next day.

It was a little Burleson magic; it's just the way he was.

"Dom [Raiola, the center] would always joke about it, 'Hey, 13, I need some Super Bowl shit today, I need some Super Bowl speeches—I need that out of you.'

"It could be a random game but he would say it to me because he needed it himself or he could feel the energy of the team and feel 'These guys are chilling right now. We need to say something that's going to spark them.' I'd talk to them like we're getting ready for the Super Bowl, and about to take the field. I'm coming with whatever is in my gut, whether I'm in tears, whether I'm smiling, whether I'm laughing, whether I'm angry. I'd tell them what I wanted. Dom would always look at me and nod, 'That was what we needed.'

"When you truly approach it like you have no other choice—we didn't want to play another week for some reason. I wouldn't say we were nervous [against the Chargers], we didn't want to leave it up to fate. We had two weeks to win one game now. We've got this week to win this game. 'If we get to next week who knows what's going to happen?' That was our message and it worked," Burleson said.

CHAPTER 14

MEL FARR

Running back, 1967–1973

The Game: November 12, 1967 vs. the Minnesota Vikings at Metropolitan Stadium

DETROIT LIONS 10, MINNESOTA VIKINGS 10

For Mel Farr, playing for the Detroit Lions became a family affair.

The running back from Beaumont, Texas, was drafted out of UCLA in the first round by the Lions in the 1967 NFL draft (seventh overall).

He played for the Lions through the 1973 season when injuries took a toll.

Mel Farr played with his older brother Miller Farr, a cornerback, during the 1973 season in Detroit. It was Miller's ninth and final season in the NFL. He only played that one season for the Lions after spending the previous eight with Denver, San Diego, Houston, and St. Louis.

The brothers grew up in the "Golden Triangle" around Beaumont, Texas, that had produced its share of football greats including Al LaBlanc, Bubba Smith, Buck Buchanan, Jerry LeVias, Warren Wells, and others.

The Farrs were heavily recruited from Hebert High School where Mel Farr excelled in baseball, basketball, track, and football.

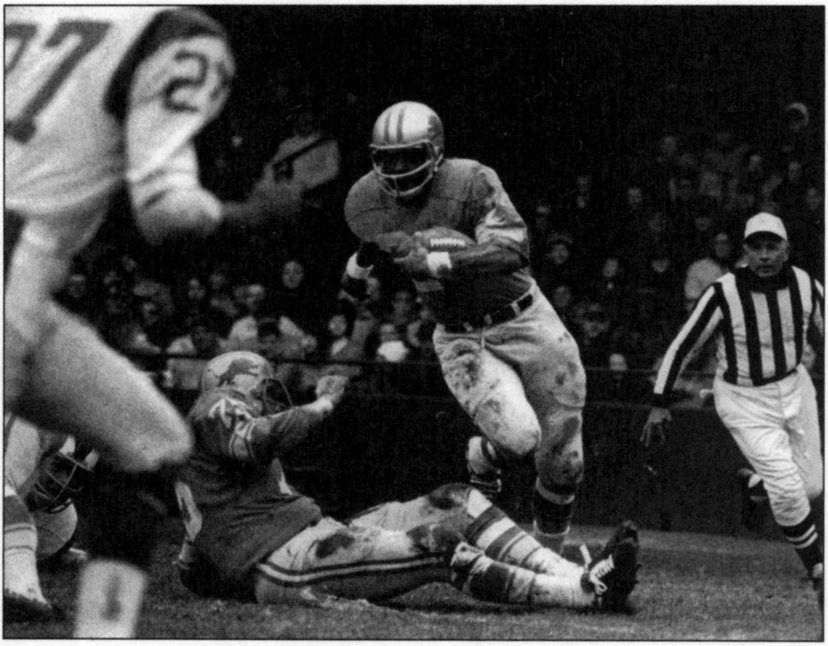

Running back Mel Farr gained 197 yards in one game as a rookie earning him the NFL's Offensive Rookie of the Year award. *Photo courtesy of the Detroit Lions*

Mel went to UCLA (although he came close to choosing Michigan State) while Miller played football and ran track at Wichita State.

So for Mel's sons it seems football was just part of their DNA.

Mel Farr's son Mike, who graduated from suburban Detroit's Brother Rice High School, played at UCLA like his father.

Mike Farr spent three seasons with the Lions (1990–92) and wore No. 81. A wide receiver, he's one of the few Detroit Lions in recent history who can claim to have played in two playoff games in the same season. After the 1991 season, Mike Farr started in the Lions' 1991 divisional round playoff game when they beat the Cowboys 38–6. Then he went on to play in the loss at Washington the next week. In those two postseason contests he had 11 catches for 135 yards. In his three seasons with the Lions he played in 42 total games with 30 starts. He had 69 receptions for 716 yards and one touchdown.

Mel's oldest son, Mel Farr Jr., played one season in 1989 for the Los Angeles Rams after he was a ninth-round draft pick by the Denver Broncos out of UCLA. Obviously, playing for the Bruins had become a family tradition after Mel Farr Sr. was a consensus All-American at UCLA in 1966.

Mel Farr's most memorable game for the Lions came to him in a snap. He was interviewed in October 2014, nine months before his sudden death on August 3, 2015.

The Game

By Mel Farr

It was his rookie season and this game stood out for one reason. "I gained 197 yards [in the game] as a rookie and it was the rookie rushing record. So I've got to be proud of that," Farr said.

"I came in, now we are all athletes, I came in [and] I thought I was the best in the game. I was the seventh pick and I thought that I should have been the first pick," Farr said with complete confidence.

"I had a little chip on my shoulder, so I said, 'You know what? I'm going to go out and prove it to them that I should've been the No. 1 pick.' I was rookie of the year so I guess I showed them."

That day at the old outdoor Metropolitan Stadium it was 42 degrees at game time, but Farr was hot throughout. He had 24 carries for 197 yards along with a pair of catches for 10 yards.

It was amazing that the Lions were able to finish with a tie considering they fumbled the ball eleven times (an NFL record) and lost five of them.

In his best single game with the Lions, Farr was only responsible for losing one fumble, although he fumbled three times. He also dropped a pass—it slipped out of his hands—when he was all alone and could've possibly scored a game-winning touchdown.

His teammate Tom Nowatzke pitched in 13 carries for 55 yards and two catches for 21 yards that day.

The Vikings scored 10 points in the second quarter. Then coming out after halftime, the Lions put 10 points on the board in the third quarter on a 26-yard pass from Karl Sweetan to Bill Malinchak. Wayne Walker also kicked a 12-yard field goal.

Another rookie, cornerback Lem Barney, also did double duty punting four times for 146 yards and returning one punt.

The rookies made quite a pair. When 1967 came to an end, Farr was named the NFL's offensive rookie of the year while Barney was the NFL's defensive rookie of the year.

For years the Vikings had some sort of hold on the Lions, who had trouble winning on the road in Minnesota.

It was the same all those years ago.

"It was Minnesota back then. You know how they had that jinx on it," Farr said.

The 197 yards were the second-best running performance in the Lions' thirty-four-year history, just one yard shy of Bob Hoernschemeyer's club record in 1950 set against the New York Yanks.

And it was the most by a running back in pro football up to that point in the 1967 season.

His long runs that day were for 57 and 52 yards.

"I felt better today than I have in any game since we opened against Green Bay, but how can you feel good after a game like that," Farr told *Detroit Free Press* columnist Joe Falls.

Other Memorable Moments

Farr had broken his nose early in the season and then aggravated it in another game. He had also dealt with a leg injury. Falls commented that he'd had enough injuries to play in the Blue Cross Bowl.

Oddly enough, the Vikings could have drafted Farr but instead selected Michigan State's Clinton Jones, who did not play on offense that day. He returned two kickoffs for a total of 27 yards.

Despite having the two rookies of the year, the Lions finished the season 5–7–2. It was Joe Schmidt's first year as head coach.

In Schmidt's fourth season came another memorable game for Farr.

It was a 28–14 win over the Oakland Raiders at Tiger Stadium on November 26.

"That was the year we were going to the playoffs. The Raiders came in and we were able to beat them on Thanksgiving Day which is a big game," Farr said.

The Raiders jumped out to a 14–0 start in the first quarter, but the Lions had it tied by halftime.

The Lions went up 21–14 in the fourth quarter on a 6-yard pass from Greg Landry to Charlie Sanders.

"The last couple minutes I ran a touchdown so we could win it," said Farr whose 11-yard scamper ensured the win.

Perhaps Farr was one of the first to see into the NFL's future. When he started negotiations for a long-term deal he had dreams of making $1 million. Not $1 million a year, but rather as a sum amount over eight to ten years.

Those numbers turned out to be just a dream. Years later earning $1 million per year in the NFL would be on the low end of the pay scale.

It was a good time to play for the Lions in those years. They had fans all over Detroit including Marvin Gaye.

But it wasn't all fun and games.

In the NFL in those days, the paychecks weren't as enormous as they are today.

The Aftermath

Farr thought about his future after football and completed his degree at the University of Detroit during his playing days. He worked in the offseason for the Ford Motor Company in its management program.

Two years after he retired from the game in 1973 he opened his first auto dealership, Mel Farr Ford in Oak Park, a Detroit suburb.

According to HistoryMakers.com: "Targeting the inner-city population with its high credit risk, but its need for automobiles and ready financing, Farr employed a variety of creative marketing and management approaches. Purchasing additional dealerships beginning in 1986, Farr's empire grew to over thirteen dealerships and a Seven-Up Bottling Plant. By 1998, the Mel Farr Auto Group was the top African American business in the country and the thirty-third largest auto dealership in the United States."

At its peak in 1998, he had $568.4 million in revenue from eleven franchises.

Farr was one of the founders of the Minority Ford Lincoln Mercury Dealers Association and was among the first black dealers to acquire a Toyota franchise, according to the *Automotive News*. By 1998, his company had dealerships in Michigan, Ohio,

Maryland, and Texas. He also had a used-car dealership in Detroit and launched a consumer loan operation that served customers with shaky credit.

Farr became well known in Detroit for his TV ads where he turned into "Mel Farr Superstar," wearing a suit and a red cape. "Mel Farr to the Rescue" was one motto and "A Farr Better Deal" was another.

Financial problems in 2002 forced Farr to dismantle his empire.

He lived in Detroit, which he'd made his home since he was drafted in 1967. He was active in the Lions' alumni network.

Chapter 15

HERMAN MOORE

Wide receiver, 1991–2001

The Game: November 23, 1995 vs. the Minnesota Vikings at the Pontiac Silverdome

DETROIT LIONS 44, MINNESOTA VIKINGS 38

As the 10th overall pick in the 1991 draft, much was expected from Herman Moore.

While the 6-foot-4 wide receiver eventually rocked the franchise record books, he got off to a bit of a slow start his rookie season. He didn't get a start until late in the season.

Then he blossomed in the playoffs. Yes, two playoff games.

"The playoff win against the Dallas Cowboys was always special because I struggled so much my rookie year that was like my coming-out party," Moore said. "Because from then on, I started. I think I started the twelfth game when Robert Clark got hurt and we were on the road at Chicago."

This game stands out for many Lions fans even if they didn't see it because it's the last playoff win for the franchise.

"What stood out for me was quarterback Erik Kramer and the coaching staff had the confidence for me to be a starter in a playoff game and here we were against the Dallas Cowboys," said Moore, who finished that game with a half-dozen catches for 87 yards.

"I went on the next week against Washington to have a good postseason game [four catches, 69 yards] as well from a personal standpoint," Moore said. "That was really my coming out, 'Here I am arriving.'"

His touchdown against the Cowboys put the nail in the coffin for Detroit's 38–6 win.

Most NFL players remember their first score well and Moore is no different.

"My first touchdown was in the right corner of the end zone one-on-one. I want to say it was against Ken Gant. Erik Kramer saw it, threw me a little fade that became my signature play, a fade to the right corner of the end zone [for seven yards]," Moore said.

"On video you see me after I catch, I shake my head like, 'I could've been doing this all season long.' I knew it was always there. I think I let a lot of people down early, because I didn't come through. And I had to fight and claw my way back. I did well in practice, but after my first preseason game in the Silverdome my rookie year, they never had confidence in me as a starter."

In the preseason Moore dropped too many balls because he couldn't see. He wore contact lenses in college, but started off without them for the Lions. An eye examination pinpointed the problem.

"I was backing Robert Clark up all year, when I did go in and spell him once in a while I did OK. They were so shaken and coach Wayne Fontes really wanted to bring me along very slowly," Moore said. "Some of that was being overly conservative and basically they reserved me into a role of learning. Then when Robert Clark got hurt against Chicago. That's when I took over I think it was twelfth or thirteenth game of the season, it was an away game.

"Oh yeah, I worked hard in practice. I never gave up," Moore said. "I really did my best to get the coach to regain the confidence

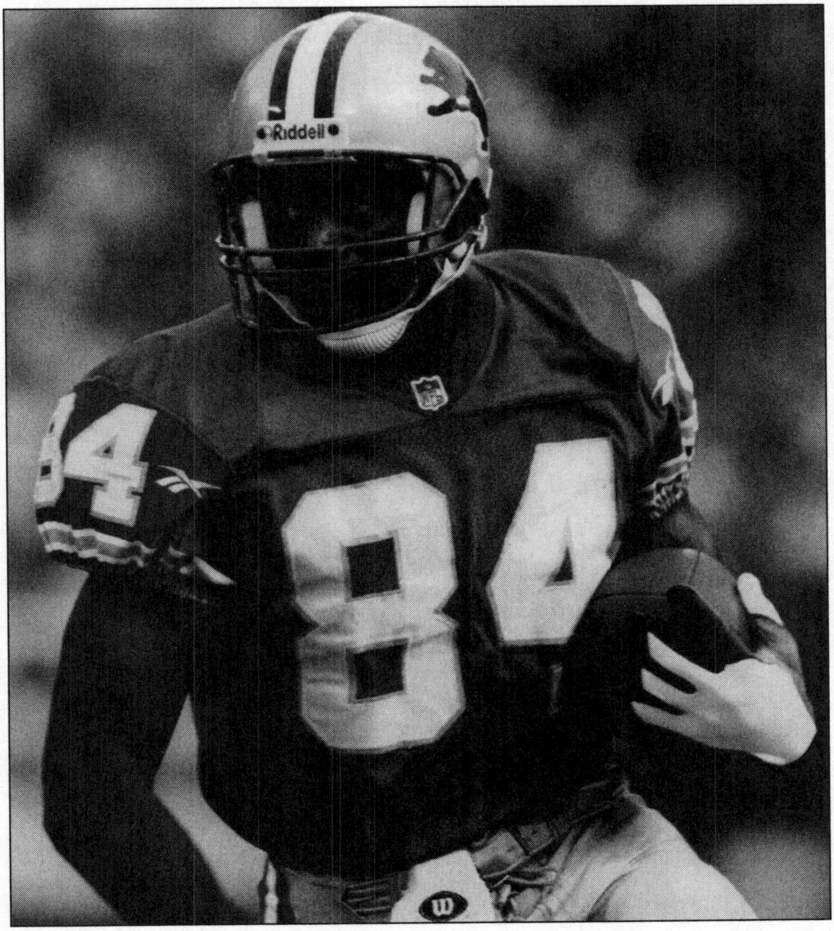

Herman Moore scored his first touchdown in the 1991 playoff win over the Cowboys at the Silverdome. *Photo courtesy of the Detroit Lions*

in me. That was just by way of practicing hard—I didn't sulk, I didn't hold my head down, I didn't do any of that. I just basically manned up, I took responsibility for having to get better. When it worked I had a lot of confidence, I was hungry. When I got in I wanted to perform. I didn't drop passes. I caught clutch passes. It was part of a tremendous 1991 season. I contributed in the final four games of the season."

Eventually he earned the trust of the coaching staff and the quarterbacks.

"Erik was vital in that he and Rodney Peete they really believed in me. The following year Rodney took over the starting position and I did well with him as well. Those two guys knew I had the ability; they always had confidence [in] me in practice. When you have that going it meant a lot because they're the guys who have to throw you the football."

That playoff win holds a special memory for Moore because it was key to his future success.

One other game stands out above the others.

By then he had found himself. In the 1995 season, he was a part of the Lions' offense that was ranked No. 1 in the NFL.

The Game

By Herman Moore

It was the Thanksgiving game where Scott Mitchell throws for 400-plus yards, Johnnie [Morton], Brett [Perriman] and myself all went for over 100. Barry [Sanders] rushed for over a hundred.

I don't know what was working that day other than we really truly believed in the offensive system we were in.

Barry Sanders is a freak of nature because he had 1,500 yards every year he played. He was always going to have his yards. To bring along a total team effort, where you can truly say, "Listen we have our entire offensive weapons involved," that was special. I've never been associated with a game like that, and I don't know how many in the history of the game have been like that where you have three receivers over 100, a running back over 100, and the quarterback throws for 400. Maybe it's more common than I realize in this day and age, but not then. [Moore had eight catches, 127 yards, one touchdown; Perriman had a dozen receptions for 153 yards and a pair of touchdowns; Morton had seven catches for 102 yards and a touchdown; Sanders carried 24 times for 138 yards and a touchdown; while Mitchell threw for 410 yards with four touchdowns and one interception.]

It turned into a shootout. What was surprising, everything seemed to click. It wasn't that Minnesota was a bad team or anything of that nature, as much as it was this was truly where we all were, you get everyone pushing. In a skill position it's always tough [when] you get all the guys pushing for each other you can equally satisfy. They always say there's not enough balls to go around, but truly this game proved that there was.

It wasn't anything that happened during the course of the game. You don't realize how well you're doing—you are not paying attention to that—you're actually doing everything to help your teammates.

We all benefited from really being unselfish. That was the game; I know we're all very unselfish players. How often do you say you're not complaining about the ball and you're not asking for it, but yet you're being productive because your teammates are helping you be productive and everyone in that phase—myself, Barry, Johnnie, Brett—we all say that about each other.

It was definitely special because it was a Thanksgiving Day game. I think it was one where we all shared a turkey that had about fifteen legs on it.

It was John Madden's thing. You usually have two guys who had the best day and they share. We had five guys—you've got

Scott, Barry, Herman, Johnnie, and Brett. It was just a big game for us all.

Other Memorable Moments

By that time Scott Mitchell and Moore had developed a solid rapport.

"Scott Mitchell was almost immediate in playing well together [with me]. I was in my third or fourth year when he came in, in 1994. I was already making tremendous strides and what was interesting, I was a little nervous about him being a left-handed quarterback because I'd never caught a football from a lefty. It turned out to be the easier pass for me to catch for some reason, being on the right side most of the time. We immediately started to click. We worked a lot one-on-one in practice; we worked a lot on just things on our own. We became very effective at the fade route—really [it was an] instinctive play that he and I had."

Both Moore and Mitchell agree that they invented the back-shoulder catch.

"One hundred percent we were the originators. What we worked on they call it back-shoulder fade stop. We called it a read fade," Moore said. "What we would do is if I got on top of the defensive back, he could throw it on top. If he knew the guy was going to stay on top of me and stay ahead of me, I knew it was coming on my back-side shoulder. We never had to think about it, we never had to talk about it. We did it so effectively the coach just allowed us to run fade routes or takeoff routes to run whoever we wanted. It could be anywhere from 30 yards to 60 yards.

"The fade for us became a high-percentage play. Unlike now the shorter guys they still have to get open, some of the bigger receivers you can see them it's all about them trying to outrun guys. That's not really what a fade should be. What we worked on is how to get the completion consistent and how to take advantage of one-on-

one coverage, that's the basic fundamental of the fade route," Moore said.

Moore wanted the defensive backs nearby.

"I wanted them really close so I could very easily manipulate them, and also I had a better view of what the pass was going to be since I was taller. A defensive back's confidence comes in knowing where you and the football are at the same time. The closer the defensive back is to me, the less he is instinctive and aware; now he's in an uncomfortable position."

It was a theory that worked. Moore went to four straight Pro Bowls from 1994 to 1997. He played eleven seasons for the Lions (1991–2001) and then briefly for the New York Giants (2002).

Moore's name is still in the Lions record books.

He holds the record for most career receptions with 670 and most receptions in a season with 123. He also is tied with Calvin Johnson for most receptions in a game with 14.

Moore is now second to Calvin Johnson for most career receiving yards. Johnson had 10,405 yards following the 2014 season, while Moore had 9,174. Moore (1,686) is also second to Johnson (1,964) for most receiving yards in a season.

Moore said it doesn't bother him that Johnson broke so many of the records he once held.

"It's a different day and age, you can look at everything from utilization, to the type of players and that's nothing to take away from the guys we see in coverage but believe me they're a far cry from Rod Woodson, Carnell Lake, Steve Atwater, and the John Lynches. It's just different," Moore said.

"You've got a few guys like Darrell Green but they don't possess the instincts. Every week you're facing typically somebody that's top-notch. And you're now in such a pass-happy league it starts with the pass and ends with the pass, they sit back and get what they get," Moore said. "Unless you've got [Seahawks running back] Marshawn Lynch or one of these teams that are very committed to the run. They know there's a tremendous gap in the ability of the defensive backs these days. They're just not the same. That's where really the weakest links are if you look at secondary, who are you going to look at and go, 'Wow that's a shutdown secondary that can challenge anybody.' To find that in this day and age . . .

"It's different you're not sharing the ball with Brett Perriman, Johnnie Morton, Barry Sanders, and, in some ways, [tight end] David Sloan," Moore said.

Certainly, Moore admires Calvin Johnson.

"I respect him and I would expect and hope he would have the same for me, which he seems to demonstrate," Moore said.

"I don't think you can take anything away from him, but I also will always defend my position. We're drastically different players, I think you can toss a quarter up and say who would you choose to be the better receiver, if people want to debate it like that. I still look at what I did and no one, including Calvin, can take that away.

"We're two different receivers," Moore said. "I played on every part of the field. He's more vertical. He's not going to be used the way I was used."

The Aftermath

As is true for for many Lions, being drafted by Detroit changed the direction of Moore's life.

"I come from very humble beginnings. I grew up in a housing project in Virginia. When I got drafted I had a mother who worked two jobs and who was struggling and trying to make ends meet," Moore said. "I was on a full scholarship at the University of Virginia. . . . When I got drafted I knew financially some things would change. I had to depend on so many people. We didn't come from a family that understood finances and how to manage those. We were really at the mercy of people we had to trust."

It all worked for Moore who has made Detroit his home.

He may have retired from football, but he's got his businesses and remains active in the community.

"Right now, I love coffee so I've stayed involved with that through licensing contracts with the Lions, the NFL, the Pro Football Hall of Fame for a specialty coffee line utilizing players and Hall of Famers," Moore said. The coffee line is called "Collectible Beans."

Legend's Roast featuring Moore on the package is advertised as "full-bodied, earthy and robust" while Hall of Fame Roast with Barry Sanders on the package is "floral, intense, chocolate." Hall of Fame roast with Charlie Sanders is "earthy, licorice, and roasty."

"I also have a video production company where we do a lot with online media engagement and also production for corporate partners," Moore said. "And the last piece is software technology. They really go hand in hand. We use the coffee as marketing collateral. The software and technology development is something we've been working on for both the amateur and professional athletics."

"We stay very busy we've had some really great relationships. I do a lot of public speaking and private speaking engagements," Moore said. "I work a lot with media so I really tie up a lot of my time through various ventures."

He can also be seen in a public service announcement for "Game On, Cancer" for the Henry Ford Health System.

He's involved with pediatric cancer research with the Ally Jolie Baldwin Foundation, where he's a board member.

"I do a lot of health and nutrition through the United Dairy Industry of Michigan involving the dairy farmers of Michigan," Moore added.

He's also involved with the Lions' alumni.

"I have a very good relationship with the Lions. Over the years it went from being one that was bitter because of the way things ended. I just really felt the cards could have been dealt a little differently—if they didn't want me here versus just having me here for security but it ruined my career," Moore said.

In his last season in Detroit in 2001, he played in three games and had just four catches for 76 yards.

"After a while it took me just maturing and becoming a bigger party to close that gap and to heal that wound because it just didn't need to be that way," Moore said. "Since then we've talked about it, they knew exactly where I stood and how I felt. I've repaired not only that relationship but others that I had with former coaches—we didn't see eye-to-eye at the time. We've become closer friends after the game."

Moore makes regular appearances at the Lions practice facility during the season, watching film for his spots on Detroit area Lions' TV shows.

"I really like coach Jim Caldwell and I like everything he has presented himself to be," Moore said. "He has done a great job helping this team grow up, and really be in charge and responsible for their own accountability. In the past that had to be policed by the coaches and by teammates. But right now he says, 'Listen, as each individual let's take the pressure off one another. Police yourself, be accountable for yourself, and stand for something, show that you're a man of character.' That's what I think we've seen."

That is what Lions fans saw from Herman Moore for eleven seasons.

Chapter 16

ROBERT PORCHER

Defensive end, 1992–2004

The Game: September 6, 1992 vs. the Chicago Bears at Soldier Field

CHICAGO BEARS 27, DETROIT LIONS 24

Like so many of the former Lions, Thanksgiving games were memorable to long-time defensive end Robert Porcher.

"There was nothing like it. Back then I think it was just really unique, you only had one game," Porcher said. "Now Thursday night football has watered that down."

One Thanksgiving in particular stood out for him.

"The first time I got a Turkey Leg Award from John Madden [which goes to the most valuable player on Thanksgiving Day], I knew everybody was watching. I think we played Chicago I can't remember exactly what year. I got it a couple times, but that was the first year. I got it, Johnnie Morton got it. I think Gus Frerotte was there too. I was so excited I actually took the bone home from one of the legs, I had it in my freezer for years. I don't know what happened to it. It was special."

A little research shows that game was in 1999. Along with Porcher, Morton, and Frerotte, running back Greg Hill also shared in the Turkey Leg Award. The Lions beat the Bears 25–21 that day.

It was a special memory, but not the most memorable for Porcher.

Without hesitation, he said the game that still stands out for him was his first regular season game as a rookie.

He didn't start and he didn't make it on the stat sheet either. He got no credit for his almost-sack of Jim Harbaugh.

It was his welcome-to-the-NFL game, and when it was over he wasn't sure he'd be invited back.

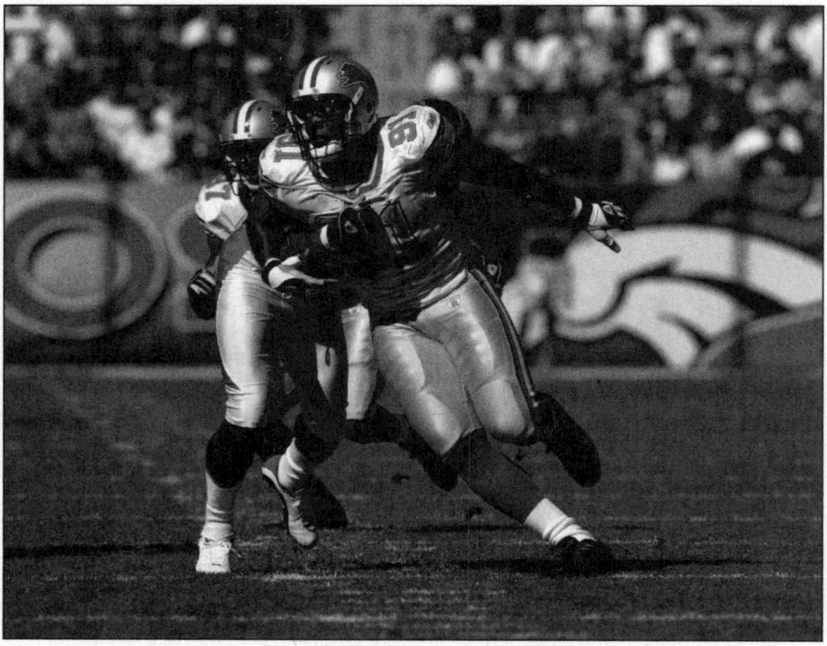

Robert Porcher, who played for thirteen seasons, thought he would be cut after his first game as a rookie. *Photo courtesy of the Detroit Lions*

The Game

By Robert Porcher

It was September of 1992. We opened up in Chicago against the Bears. Of course I'd played in preseason games [but] when I stepped on the field, my legs were frozen in place. I looked over in the end zone and saw Richard Dent, I saw Steve McMichael, I saw Mike Singletary, I saw coach Mike Ditka on the sideline. I just froze and teammate Jerry Ball came up behind me, he slapped me in my face and said, "Let's go, it's time, let's go." I was like, "Yeah, yeah."

The game, the tempo was so quick, so fast compared to the preseason. At the end of the game, Jim Harbaugh was the quarterback and they were going down to score, I came around and grabbed him, but I missed him. He shook me off and he ran, threw the ball, scored the touchdown and we lost the game.

A reporter was talking to me after the game. I was just like, "I lost the game, I should have made the sack." I was like "They're probably going to get rid of me." I remember Wayne [Fontes] saying, "I hope you rented."

That memory just stood out because I was so distraught that we lost the game. I thought it was me, but really in essence it wasn't. Back then it seemed like it, not having an experience.

It was my first game.

The Bears. The history there. Ditka.

Then in that game, Barry Sanders had one of his most memorable runs. It was an off-tackle [43-yard] play. Any time I see it I always say, "See, I'm standing right there." I say that to this day. They gave him an off-tackle play, Mike Singletary hit him, as they hit him he just kind of ran over the guys. Barry froze his eyes like that and he spun out of it and he was gone to the end zone. I just remember seeing Singletary and McMichael just stand there and shook their heads. I grabbed the guy next to me and said, "Did you see that? Did you see that?"

It was incredible.

Other Memorable Moments

It was quite an introduction to the NFL for Porcher that day.

His memory is quite good. When he missed the sack on Harbaugh, the Bears quarterback escaped and threw a six-yard touchdown pass to Tom Waddle. One second remained on the clock and the Bears had a 27–24 edge.

Talk about roller-coaster games; the Lions had taken a 24–17 lead with just 1:12 remaining on a 27-yard pass from Rodney Peete to Willie Green.

It was Barry Sanders' 43-yard run that kept the Lions in the game.

Of course Porcher, a first-round pick in 1992 out of South Carolina State, was welcomed back after his first game as a rookie.

Everyone has to get started some time and the defensive end was just getting his footing.

He became one of the NFL's dominant pass-rush specialists and was a defensive leader for the Lions for most of his thirteen years in Detroit (1992–2004).

The Aftermath

Porcher finished his career with 95.5 career sacks, a franchise record that still stands today. He still ranks fourth in sacks per season with 15. Al "Bubba" Baker holds spots 1, 2, and 3. When Porcher retired in 2004, the only two other active NFL players with more sacks were Michael Strahan with 117 and Simeon Rice with 97.

The three-time Pro Bowler (1998, 2000, and 2002) led the Lions in sacks in eight seasons and had 24 career games with more than one sack. He also had 673 tackles.

Porcher, who spent his entire career with the Lions, played 187 games and rarely missed time due to injury. In his first ten seasons, he missed two games, and then missed just three games in 2002 and 2003.

Just as emotional as his NFL debut against the Bears was his announced retirement on November 1, 2004.

He had been a healthy scratch for every game that season and couldn't take it any longer.

While it was the Lions who released him, Porcher made it clear it was a mutual decision. After thirteen NFL seasons he had to say goodbye.

"I've thought about this day for a lot of the last three years. We all think we can play forever, and I was no different, but now the time has come to step aside," Porcher said at a press conference as reported by the Associated Press.

Porcher already had announced that 2004 would be his final season, but he was counting on playing, not watching.

"These last seven weeks have been tough. I had always been proud of being part of the solution, not part of the problem," Porcher said that day.

He had no desire to play for another NFL team after spending his entire career in Detroit.

"I could never play for anyone else—I'm a Detroit Lion," he told the Associated Press. "I just appreciate that I'm being allowed to say goodbye on my own terms, not being pushed out the door."

Porcher was heavily involved in the community during his playing days and even for several years after he retired. That's why the Lions changed the name of their Man of the Year Award to the Robert Porcher Award after he won it two years in a row in 2002 and 2003.

Porcher spent time volunteering with organizations like The Heat and Warmth Fund, the Police Athletic League, and the Skillman

Foundation. He also teamed up with the University of Michigan Comprehensive Cancer Center, in 2000, to start the Porcher Cancer Relief Fund. The fund is designed to provide financial assistance to families who have children receiving treatment at the UMCCC.

Porcher, who is now retired in Orlando, also won the Lions' NFL Walter Payton Man of the Year Award for 2002 and 2003, the Detroit Lions Ed Block Courage Award for 2003, and the NFL Extra Effort Award.

It all started as he ran out of the tunnel, that early September day in 1992.

CHAPTER 17

LUTHER ELLISS

Defensive tackle, 1995-2003

The Game: December 21, 1997 vs. the New York Jets at the Pontiac Silverdome

DETROIT LIONS 13, NEW YORK JETS 10

Football is a game of emotions, which was a good fit for defensive tackle Luther Elliss.

In his nine seasons of playing for the Detroit Lions, one game stood out.

And actually, it was not the result that made it memorable. Elliss had to stop and think about whether the Lions had pulled out the win in the final game of the 1997 season before reaching the conclusion, "I think we won."

Yes they did.

After going down 10–0 after the first quarter, the Lions fought back and scored the game-winning touchdown on a 15-yard Barry Sanders scamper in the fourth quarter.

The game late that afternoon at the Pontiac Silverdome offered the best and worst of the NFL.

Barry Sanders, a future Hall of Famer, was aiming to become just the third running back in NFL history to run for 2,000 yards.

And, in an instant, linebacker Reggie Brown's life was changed forever.

Elliss had the best and worst view at the Silverdome, which was full to the rafters with 77,624 fans.

The game was so loud that the officials twice threatened to call a penalty on the Lions' defense because it was too loud for the Jets' offense to operate.

It was a game that nearly was not completed because of a severe injury to Reggie Brown, stopping the game for several minutes until he was taken off the field in an ambulance.

"I talked to the officials and they said they had been in contact with the league office and that we would continue playing the game. At that point, I gathered the team and told them we had to finish strong and that if they were a praying person, the best thing they could do for Reggie Brown was to pray," Lions coach Bobby Ross said the next day, per the *New York Times*.

It was a game that Elliss remembers to this day even though it was not about him.

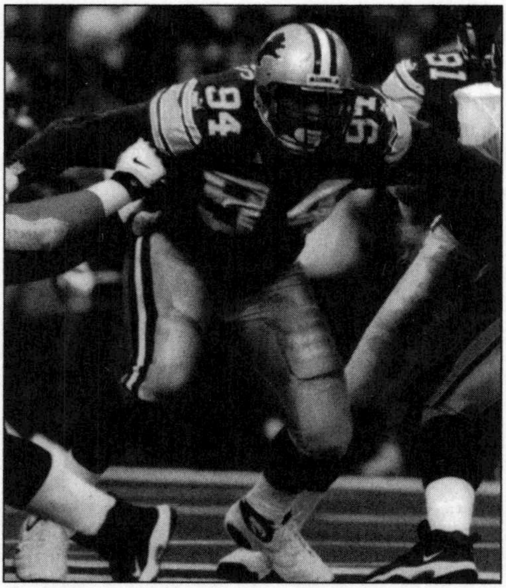

Luther Elliss played for nine seasons in Detroit and didn't hesitate when asked his most memorable game. *Photo courtesy of the Detroit Lions*

The Game

By Luther Elliss

That was versus the Jets, that was the big game when Barry goes over that 2,000 mark, the O-line is rocking and rolling, moving people, he's getting off and doing his thing.

We went from where the turf is vibrating literally on the field because of the noise level—the decibels were outrageous to how loud it was—to a dead silence all within an instant when linebacker Reggie Brown was knocked unconscious. He was down for what seemed like forever [seventeen minutes].

You talk about an emotional roller coaster—games usually are already—that was an unprecedented emotional roller coaster.

Brown's incident happened early in the fourth quarter of his 32nd and final game with the Lions.

A teammate, really without what the docs did, without what Kent [Falb, head athletic trainer] did on the field to get him breathing again. He could have died right there on the field. For sure I think that's the most memorable. There [have] been great victories, great wins, playing against some great players and things of that nature. But that was probably the most memorable one.

That's the one I tell the story the most on because it was such an extreme of high, low, and that whole thing coming together was unbelievable.

I think we won.

[With the win the Lions were in the playoffs; with the loss the Jets were knocked out. Sanders needed 131 yards to hit the 2,000-yard rushing mark and become just the third NFL player to do so.]

Barry's record was one of those things in kind of hushed tones you talked about a little.

At that time we didn't want that to be the main focus or the main emphasis of what we were doing, but it was such a huge part of it, for him to be that close.

As a defense we didn't want to sit down. Naturally we didn't want to sit down because of who he is and what he would do. "OK, Coach, I want to watch [Barry on] the Jumbotron" because he could do everything at a moment's notice.

He's probably the most gifted athlete I've ever seen. What was so great about Barry is his humbleness, just his demeanor, who he is, how he carries himself. He's truly an amazing human being and person. What he did on the field was amazing. Who he was off the field was greater.

After the game it was ecstatic, watching the guys pick up and hoist Barry. Just to be in the locker room. It was an ecstatic locker room. I know we won.

At the same time there was a concern for Reggie. We didn't really know what was going to happen, what was going on. Just that he stopped breathing, or had a hard time. It was a huge concern.

There was a joy again, but it was just a weird emotional experience because of that. We were so excited for what Barry did, we were excited for that but by the same token we were like "What's going on with Reggie?" That was one of our top concerns.

Other Memorable Moments

The players were told not to visit Brown in the hospital that night but saw him within days.

"I am worried most about his family," Sanders told reporters after the game. "We lost a teammate for a while, but I just hope that his family is OK. This really puts things in perspective."

"Actually going to see him in the hospital was a huge blessing," Elliss said. "It was comforting just to see him there. To see him acknowledge; we couldn't have a conversation. It was right after he had his halo put on, that's when I saw him. He was positive. It wasn't a deep, long conversation because he was still in and out of it but it was good."

He was assisting on a tackle of Jets' running back Adrian Murrell but the 300-pound offensive lineman Lamont Burns fell onto Brown's helmet, which jarred his neck.

His breathing stopped and, according to multiple reports, his face turned purple.

An ambulance was in place in the tunnel near the locker room, on the opposite side of the field while doctors and trainer attended to Brown immediately. Players felt helpless. Wide receivers Herman Moore and Johnnie Morton rushed to the tunnel and rolled the stretcher out to Brown before the ambulance made its way onto the field.

While there was certainly reason for concern, Brown was eventually diagnosed with a spinal cord contusion. He had surgery to fuse his first and second vertebrae. He was only twenty-three and in top physical condition, which helped his recovery. Indeed, his football career was over but he was able to live a normal life.

With the ambulance gone, the Jets (who were down 13–10) continued their drive until Neil O'Donnell had a pass intercepted by Bryant Westbrook.

When the Lions took over they couldn't get past the Jets' 43-yard line and were forced to punt. Elliss and the Lions' defense forced the Jets to punt on their next drive giving the Lions the ball at their own 42. Sanders still had time to reach his goal and he wasted no time. On the first play he ran for two yards to hit the 2,000-yard mark. The head official gave him the ball and he was mobbed by teammates as the fans again reached new decibel levels for the Silverdome. Sanders went to the sideline, tossed the ball to his father, and then went back to the huddle, back to work.

On the next play he ran 53 yards up until the two-minute warning, finishing with 2,053 yards for the season and 184 yards for the game.

Quarterback Scott Mitchell took a knee three times and an emotional game was complete.

For Elliss and the rest of the team, their season was not over. They had to prepare to play the Buccaneers at Tampa in the playoffs.

It was a day that will live in the memories of not just Elliss but everyone on the field, in the seats and in the press box.

"If you ask anyone on this team, they would be willing to give up the 2,000 yards and the victory and the playoffs to have Reggie healthy," offensive guard Jeff Hartings told the *New York Times*. "Every day I'm out there on the football field, I'll be thinking about Reggie Brown."

The Aftermath

As for Elliss, he played six more seasons for the Lions. His last season in the NFL was with the Denver Broncos in 2004.

The defensive tackle, who was a first-round draft pick (20th overall) in 1995, has gone public with financial difficulties following his playing career, during which he earned more than $11 million.

"The Lions did a good job. They put on financial programs that we had to attend, [where they talked] about investing and saving money, gave statistics on how many of us would be broke," Elliss told the Associated Press in 2010. "Guys were saying, 'It's not going to be me, I'm too smart for that.' And here I am, one of those guys."

He filed Chapter 7 bankruptcy in June 2010 due to poor decisions and bad business investments. He and his wife lost houses in Utah and Oakland Township, Michigan.

Elliss was a subject of a *60 Minutes* report. He shares his story hoping others listen and don't make the same mistakes. He spoke to Detroit Lions rookies during training camp in 2014 and he's a regular at NFL rookie symposiums.

"I talk about not being prideful. A lot of my demise came because I was prideful," Elliss said in August 2014. "I couldn't admit that I needed help. And I didn't take advantage of the resources here, and didn't let anyone know until after the fact [that I needed help]. It's those types of things, you don't need to do on your own."

Elliss, a two-time Pro Bowler who had 29 career sacks, lives in Utah with his wife and twelve children (seven adopted). He works at Operation Exchange, a sports firm in Utah.

CHAPTER 18

EDDIE MURRAY

Kicker, 1980–1991

The Game: November 15, 1981 vs. the Dallas Cowboys at the Pontiac Silverdome

DETROIT LIONS 27, DALLAS COWBOYS 24

It is amazing that sometimes NFL coaches know exactly what they are doing.

It was that way with the Lions special teams coach Joe Madden in the 1981 season. Somewhere around mid-October he started a new drill in practice.

Kicker Eddie Murray, who was in his second of a dozen seasons with the Lions, remembers it well.

"He started practicing what it would take if we had no timeouts and how much time we would actually need to run a play. The ball gets spotted, the field goal unit runs on, and the other players run off—how much time that would take to kick the field goal," Murray explained.

"We were practicing this. We all thought, 'What a stupid drill.' Everybody kept saying, 'This is never going to happen, this is never going to happen.' Then here we go four or five weeks later and it happened."

So Madden was right.

Those practices—and the officials' inability to keep track of how many Lions were on the field for the final play—may have helped the Lions beat the favored Cowboys that day.

It was one of Eddie Murray's most memorable games with the Lions.

Kicker Eddie Murray (3) played a dozen seasons with the Lions but won his Super Bowl ring with the Cowboys. *Photo courtesy of the Detroit Lions*

The Game

By Eddie Murray

A game that a lot of people always comment to me about is the twelve men on the field against the Cowboys. That seems to be with the circumstances of how unusual the play was and how we got away with having twelve men on the field and didn't get caught—all of those types of things.

We were playing the Cowboys at the Silverdome. It's toward the end of the year. It was a close game. I'm not sure if the game was tied [it was] or we were 2 points behind. Eric Hipple was the quarterback and we were driving down to kick a field goal to win the game.

Back at that time the rule [for downing the ball] was you had to take a snap and throw the ball out of bounds and they would stop the clock. That was the rule in place at that time. We had no timeouts left and Eric had thrown a deep pass down the seam to one of our tight ends Ulysses Norris. Ulysses had caught the ball on the 30-yard line and with the no timeouts.

Eric, who was my holder also on the team, was running up and he was yelling, "Clock, clock!"so he could get the ball and throw it out of bounds.

Joe Madden was the special teams coach at the time. He was saying, "Field goal team run on the field and line up and kick the ball." There was this kind of Chinese fire drill going on. There were people running onto the field who would be on the field goal team and there were people on the field who were lining up to just get in position to throw the ball out of bounds. Leonard Thompson, one of the wideouts, was split out left, in a blocked out position. Ulysses Norris, who caught the pass, wasn't on the field goal team but he lined up in the tight end position because that was his position and all he heard was Eric. We are grabbing people and throwing them off the field.

I'm running on the field. Eric is going, "What are you doing?" I say, "They told me to come on and kick the ball." I'm running and yelling. He stepped back and I just stood there. I didn't take any steps. He snapped the ball back, I kicked it. We ran out of time, people were still running all over the place. So at the time I kicked the ball we had twelve men on the field. The officials had a hard time trying to count everybody because there were people going in and out. They didn't throw a flag. Dallas was yelling and screaming and we were jumping up and down for joy because we had won the game.

It was a 48-yard field goal.

If you search Eddie Murray in YouTube that's the first one they show. It's kind of identified with me because of the unusual circumstances.

There was a big picture in the *Free Press* and the *News* the next day and they had a number over everybody. There were twelve guys. They count me as the twelfth guy. I should be No. 1 because who's going to kick the ball? I'm not the odd man out. I was the one who was supposed to kick the ball. They should have made Leonard Thompson the twelfth guy. We had two or three guys who normally wouldn't be on the field. Some of the field goals guys were running on and they turned around and ran back off. They saw that guys were trying to line up and throw the ball out of bounds. It was just a cluster.

I had no time to think of the situation. No time for taking any steps. I remember running over really quickly and giving Eric the spot, jumping back and kicking the field goal, and we win. People are jumping on me, I was just enveloped in the whole aftermath of the kick.

Other Memorable Moments

Murray, who was a seventh-round draft pick out of Tulane in 1980, said the Lions were still a growing team in 1991. After going 9–7 in 1980, they finished 8–8 and second in the NFL Central.

The Cowboys were three-point favorites that day. It was one of only four losses during their 1991 season.

Billy Sims, who had 119 yards rushing that afternoon, caught an 81-yard touchdown pass from Hipple to tie the game at 24–24 and give Murray and the Lions a chance to win it. It was Murray's second of twelve seasons with the Lions.

Murray kicked one other field goal that day—from 37 yards and minus the chaos on the field.

While that game quickly came to mind as his most memorable game, he said the Lions' season that stands out the most was in 1991.

That was the year the Lions were one win away from the Super Bowl.

After beating Dallas 38–6 in the divisional round of the playoffs, they went to Washington and didn't look anything like the Lions from the previous week.

"Being a part of the 1991 12–4 year, my last season as a Lion, that was a pretty special year," Murray said. "To make it to the NFC Championship game—I was proud to be a part of that team."

While with the Lions, Murray was a two-time Pro Bowl kicker (1980, 1989) and four-time All-Pro (1980, 1981, 1982, 1989). As a rookie he was the Pro Bowl MVP.

Murray's career was far from over when he left the Lions after that 1991 season. He played in the NFL for twenty years. He went on to play for the Kansas City Chiefs, the Tampa Bay Bucs, Philadelphia Eagles, Washington Redskins (two stints), Minnesota Vikings, and two seasons with the Dallas Cowboys including the 1993 season when they won the Super Bowl.

Murray still wears his Super Bowl ring often.

"It was my fourteenth year in the league and the pure joy and excitement of winning the game, I know why I worked so hard to get to that," Murray said. "We were a game away in Detroit in '91. Some players thought it was always going to be like this. It's really not going to be always like that. The franchises we know that are pretty consistent in the playoffs—New England, San Francisco, and the Cowboys teams. There are thirty-two teams; a lot don't get a chance to go back.

"For me to have a chance to play in that next game was really special. I still wish it said Detroit Lions on it, it means a lot to me. I had a big part in the season, I went there [to Dallas] early in the year and I had some crucial kicks for them. They were such a great team, it was very enjoyable to play with them."

The Aftermath

No matter where he traveled in the NFL, Detroit was always home.

He grew up in Victoria, British Columbia but has lived in the Detroit area since he was a rookie in 1980.

He had a few good reasons to stay. During his playing career he was always preparing for his future without football.

"I was kind of a rarity back then. I always took a job in the offseason," Murray said. "I did a lot of sales rep or new business or some kind of a position with companies. I wore a bunch of different hats, did a bunch of different things. I did it because I was always scared I was going to lose my job. So my thing was, I'm going to build up some kind of networking or some kind of opportunity for myself when football will end, not knowing I was going to play twenty years.

"If I had known that I more than likely wouldn't have worked. That was always the attitude I had. When I retired [from football] in 2000 I just went to work again. That's what I knew [how] to do. I married a girl from Michigan. I made roots here because of staying here in the offseason. I chose not going back to Canada and just make my home here.

"Here it is thirty-five years later," Murray said. "I love living in Detroit, people in Michigan have been great, I love the state. I have no plans of going anywhere else."

Today he's in business development and outside sales for Great Lakes Wire and Cable, a copper and fiber optic wire distributor.

"We supply a lot of electrical contractors and telecommunications companies like AT&T and a lot of cell tower work," Murray said. "We don't do any installation; we just supply them with the electrical wiring."

When people meet him and hear his name especially in Michigan, they certainly remember his days with the Lions.

"Our company is a nationwide company. I do a lot of sales down in Dallas, they still remember me from playing with them in the Super Bowl year," Murray said. "Of course I wear my Super Bowl ring when I'm in meetings; that's always a good talking point."

In his spare time, Murray still occasionally gives private kicking lessons for high school and college kids.

"I help the high school kids get scholarships and some of the college kids that would like to move on and maybe get an opportunity to have a chance to kick in the pros," Murray said. "I try to give them some guidance that way and they may be able to get picked up."

He worked with Dave Rayner, who went to Oxford High School and then Michigan State before kicking stints with eight NFL teams between 2005 and 2011. Rayner kicked in eight games for the Lions in 2010 when Jason Hanson was injured.

"I was very close with [him] and helped out a lot in the early part of his Michigan State career, also in his professional career," Murray said.

Murray has kept close ties with the Lions through the years and is on the Detroit Lions Alumni Board.

"It's been really nice trying to keep the alumni connected with the active team and supporting a lot of the charity initiatives that not only the alumni association has but also the active Lions team has," Murray said.

He's on the field at least once a season.

"They have the alumni game once a year where they roll us old farts out there to wave and say hi to everybody," Murray said. "It's always like a reunion time for us; we get a chance to see guys we haven't seen for a while."

He also keeps a close eye on the Lions these days and thinks the team is headed in the right direction.

"I'm very pleased, I know last year [2014] was a very nice season for them to have especially under a new coach in the first year. In years past when we've had a coach come in,we've never had this kind of success [in his first year]," Murray said. "So it's an indication that the players are buying in and really enjoy working under coach Jim Caldwell's system on offense and defense. They got some really nice results with that. Football is a different game now. Decisions are made on money, not ability. You can't put the best team on the field you can—only put the best team you can fit under the cap . . . "

When the Lions kickers Nate Freese and Alex Henery started the season going four for 10 on field goal attempts, it was a little hard to take.

"If I was a few years younger, I would've kicked off some of the rust and got out there," Murray said.

He thinks the team is in good hands now with Matt Prater.

And, after all, Murray had twenty good NFL seasons with plenty of memories and a Super Bowl ring, too.

Chapter 19

SHAUN ROGERS

Defensive tackle, 2001–2007

The Game: November 4, 2007 vs. the Denver Broncos at Ford Field

DETROIT LIONS 44, DENVER BRONCOS 7

When Shaun Rogers had something to celebrate he'd gesture as if he was ripping off his shirt like he was Superman.

The defensive tackle certainly had his Superman moments.

None stood out like one game against the Broncos in 2007.

Superman might have been no match for Rogers that day.

First, Rogers knocked Broncos' quarterback Jay Cutler out of the game on his first sack of the day early in the second quarter. Then he mistreated backup quarterback Patrick Ramsey the rest of the afternoon.

Rogers stood 6-foot-4 and had a playing weight of around 340 pounds (at least that's what was listed in the media guide). Keeping his weight down was a perennial issue. In fact, he was suspended for four games in 2006 for using a banned weight loss supplement.

His nickname in Detroit was "Big Baby," which was better than his high school nickname, "Chunks."

The guy was strong and, for his size, had tremendous speed. Before the draft in 2001, he weighed about 320 and ran a 40-yard dash in 5.3 seconds. That's speedy for a big guy. In comparison, defensive tackle Ndamukong Suh, who weighs 30 pounds less, ran a 5.03 at the NFL Combine.

Rogers was drafted by the Lions in the second round (61st overall) in 2001.

"He's the best defensive player in the NFL. Can't block him, can't do anything to him," Rogers' teammate Roy Williams told the Associated Press after his game against the Broncos.

Rogers didn't have to think long about his most memorable game.

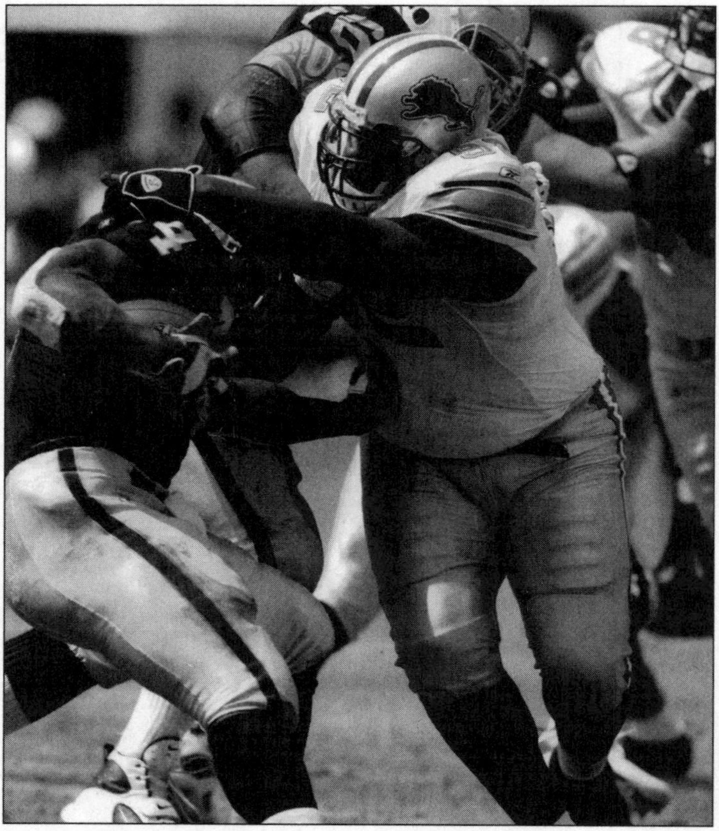

Shaun Rogers, who was known as "Big Baby" in Detroit, needed oxygen after an interception and 66-yard touchdown run. *Photo courtesy of the Detroit Lions*

The Game

By Shaun Rogers

It was a pretty memorable game for me. I had a touchdown and interception return for 66 yards. I also had like two and a half sacks.

It was a home game. We played the Denver Broncos when Jay Cutler was there, it was probably the best entire game I've had.

There wasn't a lot of that going on, we occasionally won.

Those times, we were just nose to the grind[stone]. We were just trying to make sure we always fought every week and took every week as serious and the same as possible for me.

The play for a touchdown, the quarterback [Patrick Ramsey] was trying to throw a screen pass. It may or may not have been tipped at the line, I just happened to be in the area in the back. I saw it floating and kind of smashed it out of the air. I tried to do my best J.J. Watt before J.J. Watt.

Sixty-six yards is a long haul.

Most definitely I was very, very exhausted. No doubt about it.

A young fellow ran up on me and tried to tackle me. Unfortunately, his name was Selvin Young, a former University of Texas guy. So sometimes when we get together at these U-T events being a former U-T guy myself, we have to reminisce on my infamous stiff-arm of Selvin Young on my touchdown. A lot of people couldn't catch me; I had such a lead. He was the only guy in stride range.

No celebration that day. I was on the bench with oxygen.

That play was in the fourth quarter. I played again, but my day was pretty much done after that.

Other Memorable Moments

Rogers refused to talk to reporters after that game, but his teammates and coaches had plenty to say.

Quarterback Jon Kitna (from *Detroit Free Press*): "That's the kind of player he is, and I think right now the way he's feeling and how healthy he's feeling and how good he's feeling about where this team is, you're starting to see the best of Shaun Rogers. And it's only going to get better from this point forward, I think."

Coach Rod Marinelli (from *Detroit News*): "Yeah, he was big. I mean he's been playing well. He's having a great year, a tremendous year. It's just his presence. I called him 'the server' because he keeps serving sacks for everybody because he's so disruptive. Now he's starting to be the stealer, he's starting to take them."

For his effort that day, Tom Kowalski of MLive.com gave out one of his "game balls" to Rogers: "The most dominant player on the field in this game was 'Big Baby' who had 2.5 sacks and intercepted a pass from Denver backup quarterback Patrick Ramsey and returned it 66 yards for a touchdown. Rogers is generously listed at 340 pounds in the media guide, but he's a lot closer to 400 than 300. Yet, he might be one of the best athletes on the entire roster. He didn't just run it back 66 yards, he motored. He stiff-armed poor Selvin Young of the Broncos inside the 10-yard line, sticking a paw into Young's face. Priceless! He then did a pratfall into the end zone, took a breather, which he deserved, then struck his Superman pose. Priceless! Earlier in the fourth quarter, he did a somersault after getting another sack. It was a graceful somersault, too. Priceless! After the game, he gave the media the silent treatment. He let his play on the field do all the talking. You had to respect that. In all, Mr. Rogers was one giant bundle of athletic skill and entertainment. He can have two game balls."

That win over the Broncos boosted the Lions' record to 6–2.

"This is real, what you see is what you get," defensive end Cory Redding told *The Detroit News*. "It's a different team, it's not the same old Lions no more. I'll tell you that right now."

Rogers' touchdown was one of two by the defense that day. Earlier in the game Ramsey was strip-sacked by Corey Smith and the ball recovered by Dewayne White who took it three yards for a touchdown.

Rogers was recognized for his stellar play that day as NFC defensive player of the week.

"I'm just happy to be 6–2. That type of stuff just takes care of itself when you're winning," Rogers told MLive.com after receiving the honor. "Definitely [it's fun]. You can enjoy the plays that you get a chance to make and the things you do on the field a lot more when you win. It's more fun than it's been in awhile, yeah."

Rogers played thirteen seasons in the NFL, but that was his only interception.

It wasn't, however, his only touchdown. On Christmas Eve in 2005, the Lions played the New Orleans Saints at the Alamodome in San Antonio, Texas. The game took place in the aftermath of Hurricane Katrina, which had sent the Saints to a new temporary home. Lions defensive end James Hall forced a fumble and it was recovered on the Saints' 21-yard line and run in for a touchdown by Rogers.

Rogers was drafted by the Lions in the second round in 2001—the third Lions' draft pick that day. It was the same draft in which tackle Jeff Backus was selected in the first round and center Dominic Raiola was taken earlier in the second round. It was generally considered one of Matt Millen's best draft classes.

The Aftermath

After a rift with the Lions put him on the trading block, the beefy defensive tackle was sent to the Cleveland Browns following the 2007 season for cornerback Leigh Bodden and a third-round draft pick. In that final season in Detroit, he notched seven sacks, but none in the final six games. In that six-game stretch he also had just 17 tackles (including eight solo), no forced fumbles, and no fumble recoveries.

Rod Marinelli, the Lions coach in 2007, told MLive.com: "The bottom line, at the end of the day, is that you've got to have guys doing it your way. Even if you don't play well, you've got to play hard. If you don't, you become what you tolerate. If you tolerate poor practice habits, if you tolerate not finishing, if you tolerate lack of execution, that's what you become."

Four years later in 2011, Lions general manager Martin Mayhew wished things had been different between the team and Rogers.

"I like Shaun and I wish things had been a little different," Mayhew told MLive.com on February 25, 2011. "I wish that when he was here, we could've worked things out and found a way to keep Shaun Rogers here. Locked ourselves in a room and talked it through and figured it all out. I wish it had gone a different way but it's a different time now. Nothing against him personally, but it's a different time for our franchise right now, we're in a different place."

After the trade in 2008 Rogers signed a six-year, $42 million contract with the Browns.

He played in Cleveland for three seasons (2008–2010), then spent a year with the Saints (2011), and his final two NFL seasons with the New York Giants. He missed the 2013 season due to a blood clot in his leg.

In thirteen NFL seasons, Rogers had 37.5 sacks (29 of them in his seven seasons in Detroit). He also had 513 tackles, four forced fumbles, and eight fumble recoveries. In his first five seasons in Detroit he missed only four games.

He went to the Pro Bowl twice while with the Lions, in 2005 and 2006.

Rogers is retired and lives in Houston.

In October 2014 he attended a Lions' alumni function and felt like a kid in the room. It was the first fall he hadn't played football in as long as he could remember. "I'm sitting back and trying to put this part of my life together, formulate a plan, set some goals," Rogers said.

He watches Lions games when he gets a chance.

"In my region in Texas I don't get a lot of Lions games, but I do watch them," Rogers said.

And he had been impressed with the defensive line that featured Ndamukong Suh for five seasons along with guys like Ziggy Ansah, Jason Jones, and Nick Fairley.

"I like what I see out of those guys," Rogers said.

Of course he would.

Chapter 20

DRE BLY

Cornerback, 2003–2006

The Game: November 27, 2003 vs. the Green Bay Packers at Ford Field

DETROIT LIONS 22, GREEN BAY PACKERS 14

Dre Bly won the Super Bowl as a rookie with the St. Louis Rams.

Yet four years later in 2003 when he signed as a free agent with the Detroit Lions, the cornerback seemed like a good fit. And he was.

Unfortunately for Bly, his four-year stint (2003–2006) was in the middle of a ten-year losing stretch for the Lions. The team won five games in 2003, six in 2004, five in 2005, and three in 2006. Bly loved the city, but got frustrated by the losing.

And on the day after Steve Mariucci was fired in 2005, Bly told the NFL Network that if backup quarterback Jeff Garcia had been healthy all season, the Lions would have been in a better situation and Mariucci wouldn't have been fired. His ire was targeted at Joey Harrington who struggled that season, his fourth with the Lions.

It wasn't Bly's decision to leave. He was traded in March 2007 to the Broncos for running back Tatum Bell, tackle George Foster, and a draft pick.

Bly didn't hesitate for a second when asked about his most memorable game while wearing the Honolulu blue and silver.

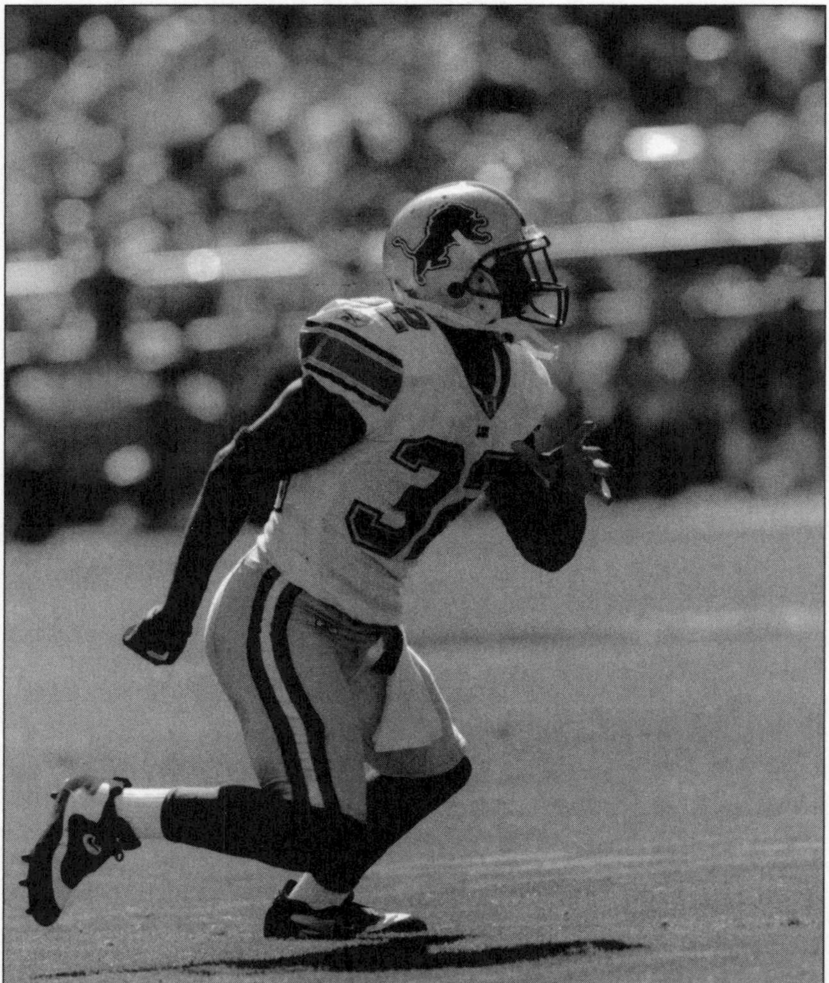

Dre Bly didn't see many wins during his four seasons with the Lions, but he loved Detroit and tried to make a comeback in 2010. *Photo courtesy of the Detroit Lions*

The Game

By Dre Bly

[The game was] in Detroit [in] 2003, my first Thanksgiving game, and it might have been one of our first wins. They hadn't had many wins since then at Thanksgiving. I think they won this past year on Thanksgiving. [Actually the Lions lost nine straight on Thanksgiving following the 2003 game, but won in 2013 and 2014.]

We beat Green Bay. I actually got the Gobbler Award that year. I intercepted Brett Favre two times. It was one of our first wins on Thanksgiving [the Lions had lost in 2001 and 2002] and it was against Brett Favre.

The Packers were obviously heavily favored [by 6.5 points]. It was a playoff team—they were obviously the favorite team in the NFC North. We actually played pretty well offensively. That might have been one of our most complete games that year defensively. Joey Harrington was the quarterback. We had a pretty good game offensively and defensively.

That was my first game back off a hamstring injury. Before that I had four picks. I was sort of solidifying myself as a premier corner that year. That was like my breakout year and after I played well against Green Bay and Brett Favre that game, that was the game that put me over the top. They had me No. 1 as far as fan vote for the Pro Bowl.

Both of the interceptions were in the second half—the first interception was intended for Antonio Freeman.

On my second interception, it was a seven route [a corner route]. Favre tried to throw to Donald Driver. I undercut it and caught it, ran to the sideline hobbling, tried to score and got tackled. My helmet came off. It was here at home. The fans went nuts and it was an exciting time.

I think we intercepted Brett three or four times that game. It sort of sparked us.

Other Memorable Moments

Thanks to Bly and the Lions defense it was a rough afternoon for Favre, whom Bly mentioned six times in his description of the game. Favre, who also lost a fumble, was sacked four times—twice by Robert Porcher, once by Shaun Rogers, and once by Dan Wilkinson.

It was a highlight of the season for the Lions, who were coached by Steve Mariucci. They finished 5–11 and in the basement of the NFC North while the Packers finished 10–6 and won the division.

And no wonder Bly remembers it. Not only did he intercept Favre twice, the cornerback also had three pass deflections and one forced fumble.

Bly was a good fit in Detroit, but it didn't last. He'd started his career with the St. Louis Rams, who drafted him in 1999, and he won a Super Bowl with them. He signed as a free agent with the Lions in 2003 and stayed for four seasons. He played for the Broncos in 2007 and 2008 and finished his career with the 49ers in 2009.

Still, at age thirty-three he thought he had more football left in him so he signed a two-year deal with the Lions on July 2, 2010. He had a good training camp and many expected he would start at nickel. Instead, he didn't make the final cut for the 53-man roster.

He wanted that comeback to work.

Just before camp started in 2010, he told the *Sporting News*: "That's where I played my best ball. I was active in the community. If you know anything about me, you know I'm not a quitter, and when I was there I had hope, I had faith that we would turn it around. We'd have games or spurts where I thought we were on our way, and it didn't work out that way. Then I was traded off, and they had different coaches come in and stuff like that. But from what I've heard, it's a new attitude, it's a new change.

"I've been blessed, I've accomplished all my dreams, playing in Pro Bowls, won a Super Bowl, so I've done everything I needed to do. But I'm telling you, this is the way to go out, to have the chance to be back in Detroit. Coach [Jim] Schwartz has come in and changed the attitude. I've heard great things about [Matthew] Stafford, an up-and-coming strong guy. I really feel, based on what I've heard, this team is going in the right direction and I want to be a part of it."

Still, Bly is not bitter.

The Aftermath

He made an appearance at training camp in 2014 and is not a stranger when it comes to being around the team.

Clearly, he feels affection for Detroit and the Lions.

"For one, it *is* a football town. It's way more of a football town than anyplace I've been," he told the *Sporting News* in the same interview. "I think it's more of a football town than Denver is. With Michigan and Michigan State, all the diehard people in Michigan, it's a football town. They're just dying for a winner. That has to excite you being a member of the team. As many years as they've struggled, they still sell out the games. When I was there the first time, we struggled and sold out every home game just about. Fans were there—tailgating and supporting the guys. Then after two or three quarters when, you know, we weren't playing to their standards, you'd see the signs come out and hear the boos. But for the most part, they came out every Sunday and supported us."

Chapter 21

LARRY LEE

Offensive lineman, 1981–1985

The Game: November 24, 1983 vs. the Pittsburgh Steelers at the Pontiac Silverdome

DETROIT LIONS 45, PITTSBURGH STEELERS 3

Thanksgiving Day games have a special hold on many of the Lions' former players, including Larry Lee.

It was a day that for years seemed to bring out the best in the Lions, who are always guaranteed the national spotlight on that one day. It's a tradition since 1934.

In 1983 the Lions had a good season, finishing 9–7 and winning the NFC Central. The Thanksgiving Day massacre of the Steelers was by far their largest margin of victory that season. It wasn't like the Steelers were a bad team—they finished 10–6 and won the AFC division title under coach Chuck Noll.

Thanksgiving just held a little magic that day for Lee and his teammates, specifically the offense which featured quarterbacks Eric Hipple and Gary Danielson and running back Billy Sims.

While the Lions ran up 328 total yards of offense, the Steelers (playing without quarterback Terry Bradshaw) were held to 218 yards. Pittsburgh committed five turnovers and the Lions led in time of possession, holding onto the ball for 38:21.

No wonder it's the most memorable game for Lee who played eight seasons in the NFL, five of them with the Lions (1981–1985).

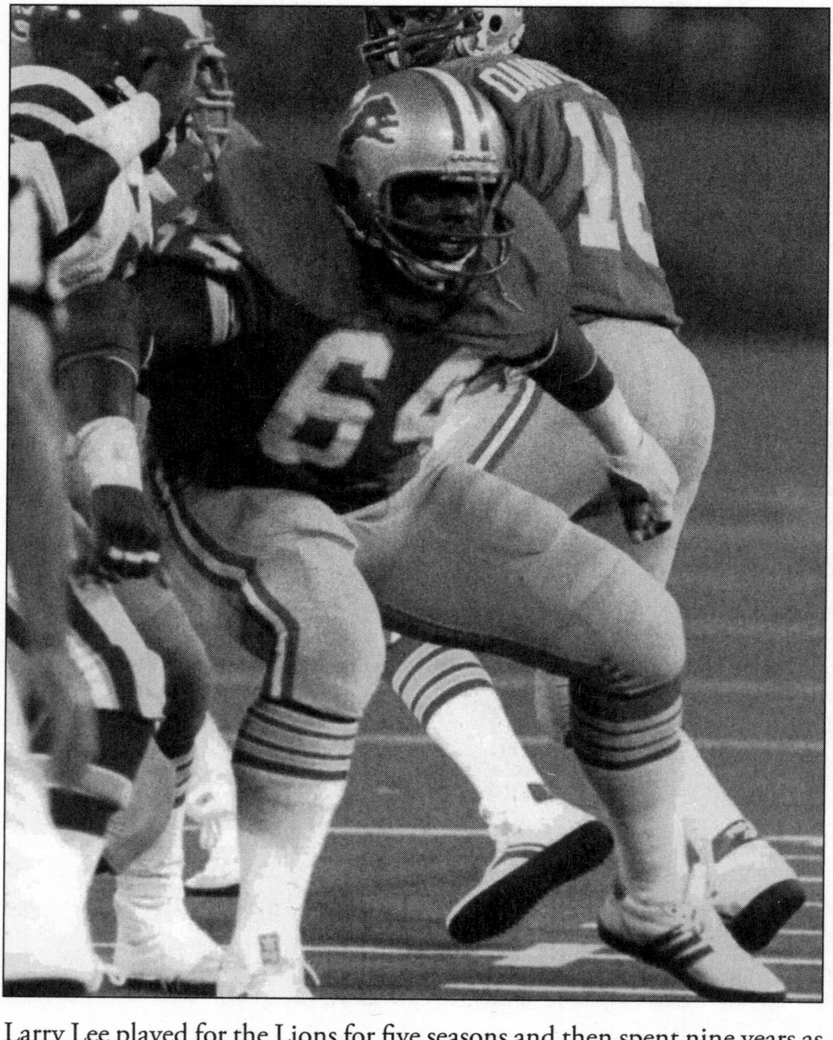

Larry Lee played for the Lions for five seasons and then spent nine years as the vice president of football operations. *Photo courtesy of the Detroit Lions*

The Game

By Larry Lee

It was Thanksgiving.

I was a third-year guy. I was starting on the offensive line, and it was [against] the Pittsburgh Steelers. They were still in their heyday. We were playing them in the Silverdome.

The day before—you know how writers have key matchups and things—one of the key matchups was Larry Lee vs. Jack Lambert. I said, "I have arrived because the writers said one of the key matchups in the game was me against Jack Lambert."

As it turned out we beat them bad that day; we beat them 45–3 or something like that. They were still a great team, but we beat them.

Billy Sims had a great day. He ran for over a hundred something [106] yards and two touchdowns.

It was just a good game all-around.

I did very well. I did well against Lambert and that great defense, [and] all those other stars.

That was back when Thanksgiving meant a little bit more than it does now. It's still an important game, it was the only one. We were playing the Steelers, they were still world-class.

They were heavily favored. I think we were around.500—we might have been 6–6.

The whole team was extra fired up, that was a special day. To beat the Steelers that day 45–3, was unbelievable and they were still a great team. The Lions we beat them up that day.

Monte Clark was the coach, Billy Sims [was the] running back, Doug English on the defensive line That was the game, my third year as a starter.

I felt better about the matchup afterward. We had a great game. I did well against him [Lambert]. We all seemed to play well that day.

Other Memorable Moments

That game prompted a famous line from Johnny Carson that night: "I'll tell you what kind of Thanksgiving I had. I had the Steelers and 41."

It was the Steelers' worst loss since 1947; hence Steelers' fans still refer to it as the "Thanksgiving Day Massacre."

The Lions scored on their first four possessions and led 24–3 at halftime.

"As I was walking back in here [to the locker room], I mulled over what was the turning point of this game was. I decided it was the opening kickoff," Chuck Noll told the Associated Press.

As bad as it was for the Steelers, it was that good for Detroit.

"We're for real. We're not making too many mistakes right now. This is a definite morale booster going into the last few games," Billy Sims told the Associated Press.

It was the first road loss in six games for the Steelers.

While the Lions usually played their best on Thanksgiving, it was not that way for the Steelers. This loss in 1983 wasn't even their worst performance in a Turkey Day game. although at the time it was. On Thanksgiving Day at Ford Field in 1998, perhaps the most memorable moment was the overtime coin toss. Pittsburgh's Jerome Bettis called tails and the official said he called heads. The Lions got the ball, drove down the field and Jason Hanson kicked the game-winning field goal.

The Lions' Thanksgiving win in 1983 was the seventh that season for the team, which finished 9–7 in the NFC Central. That was good enough for the Lions to claim their first division championship since 1957.

In the divisional playoff at Candlestick Park, the Lions lost to the 49ers 24–23 when Eddie Murray missed a 44-yard field goal with five seconds remaining.

That 1983 season was good enough that coach Monte Clark returned in 1984.

"I liked Monte. He was a good coach," Lee said who was drafted in the fifth round in 1981 out of UCLA.

"He drafted me out of college. I was like one of Monte's guys," Lee said.

Clark coached the Lions from 1978 until he was fired after the 1984 season.

"When Darryl Rogers came in and let me go. I got cut by the Lions and Monte Clark calls me at 6 o'clock in the morning. 'Hey, Larry, what happened?'

"I said, 'I guess you know, Darryl never really liked me.'

"He said 'Well, I just talked to Don Shula and the Dolphins are going to pick you up, so you'll be in Miami this afternoon.'

"I said, 'OK' and sure enough Don Shula called me. Monte was the famous offensive line coach for Shula's 1972 Dolphins—they were best friends," Lee said.

He played two seasons with the Dolphins (1985–86) and then wrapped up his playing career with the Denver Broncos (1987–1988). He played in Super Bowl XII with the Broncos.

The Aftermath

But Lee wasn't done with football. After retiring as a player, he returned to Detroit where he served as vice president of football operations for the Lions for nine years. He was responsible for the day-to-day operations of the team along with being involved with the salary cap, personnel decisions, contract negotiations, and player engagement.

Lee keeps a high-profile presence in Detroit and around Michigan these days with his band Larry Lee & the Back in the Day.

He sings and plays bass guitar, which he has played for thirty years, surrounded by former members of the Temptations, Four

Tops, Spinners, Dramatics, Contour, Funk Brothers, Dennis Edwards and his Temptation Review, and a Gospel Music Hall of Fame inductee.

They play a mix of old-school funk combined with R&B, pop, soul, blues, Motown, hip-hop, and even disco.

In 2006 Lee was named the Urban Funk Bass Player of the Year at the Detroit Music Awards.

He's also active in Detroit Lions' alumni events around the city and is one of many former Lions who made Detroit their home when their playing days were over.

He has two daughters, Dayna and Danielle. Danielle is player personnel assistant for the NFL.

Chapter 22

SCOTT CONOVER

Offensive lineman, 1991–1996

The Game: January 5, 1992 vs. the Dallas Cowboys (playoffs) at the Pontiac Silverdome

DETROIT LIONS 38, DALLAS COWBOYS 6

Scott Conover will always have something to tell his grandkids.

In the day, as an offensive lineman for the Lions, he blocked for Hall of Fame running back Barry Sanders.

"It was great blocking for Barry. He made up for it if you missed a block," Conover said. "He was a unique runner [in] that he knew if he started out on the backside, he may go to the frontside because he could change directions so quickly. He made it so easy: if you stayed with the block, he'll do the rest. He could get through the smallest seam, the smallest hole. He did a great job of setting up blocks for us."

Everyone has seen the highlights. Sanders was in a category of his own.

But it wasn't just the number of rushing yards he accumulated.

"He also made it easy when we had to pass block. They [the defense] always had to account for him in the backfield. You could see the defensive linemen take a little quick peek in there to see if Barry had the ball," Conover said. "Every little second counts; that helped us out. It was awesome blocking for him."

On pass plays, Sanders pitched in too.

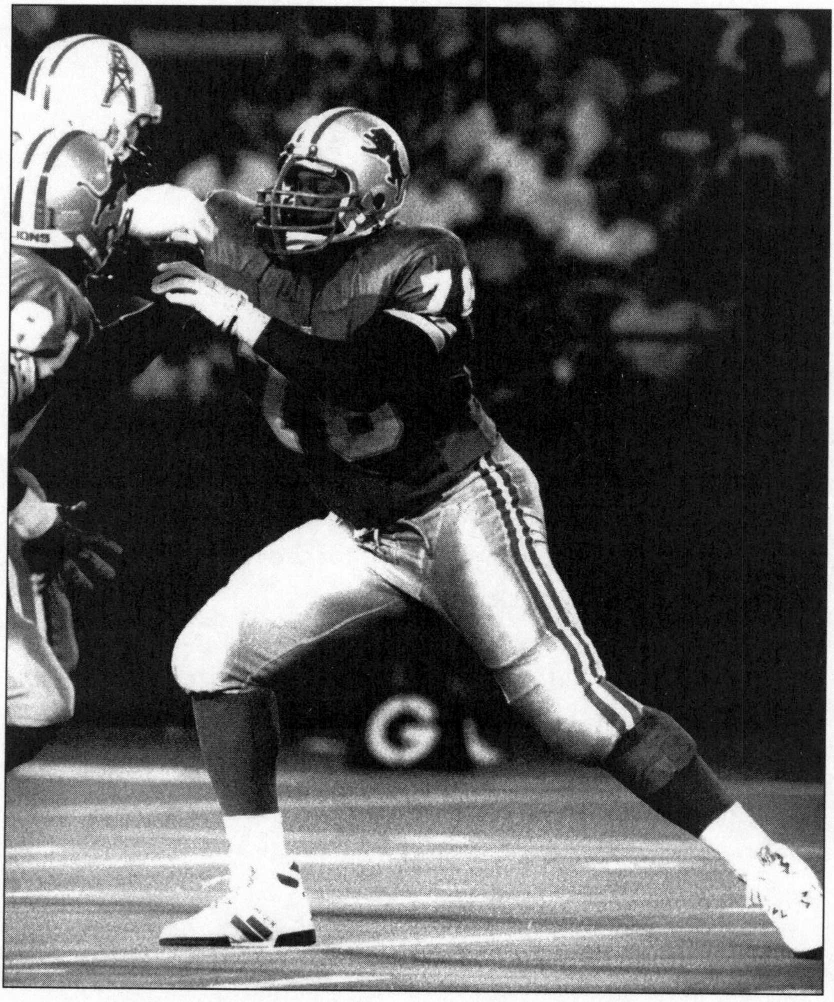

Scott Conover counts blocking for Barry Sanders as the highlight of his Lions career. *Photo courtesy of the Detroit Lions*

"He was part of the protection. We rarely had tight-end sets. We had four wide receivers, five linemen, and then Barry in the backfield. He was really good at picking up blitzing linebackers. People think of him just as a runner but he was really good at picking up blitzes. He was definitely part of the passing packages in the protection."

So it should come as no surprise that when the Dallas Cowboys were planning for the divisional playoff game against the Lions, they were keyed in on Sanders. Their goal was to keep him quiet. They succeeded for more than three quarters.

What the Cowboys didn't count on was that quarterback Erik Kramer (29–38, 341 yards, three touchdowns) would torch the Cowboys defense while Dallas quarterbacks Steve Beuerlein and Troy Aikman could not get the Dallas offense in gear with two interceptions and zero touchdowns between them.

Conover played for the Lions for six seasons—67 games and 27 starts.

It's easy to see why this playoff game—the Lions' first since 1983—was so memorable.

The Game

By Scott Conover

I was a rookie and I actually started that game at right tackle. That last string of regular season games we won all the way through until the playoffs. We had that long streak of six straight wins.

Having that playoff game at home, being a rookie, seeing how the team was excited about finally making it to the playoffs. It was the first time in I don't know how many years. Not just that, but to host a game was great.

The atmosphere was electric. I'd never experienced anything like it.

We felt good about going in there. We had played the Cowboys earlier in the year and I believe we won also (34–10 in Week 9). We felt good. We won the last six games and the last two games were on the road [at Green Bay and at Buffalo].

It was the last time we won at Green Bay. It's been a while now on the road. We were high on those wins. I believe we had to wait for Chicago to lose the Monday night game and that happened. So we clinched the division and that made us get a home game and a first-round bye.

I remember everything was clicking that day. We were moving the ball up and down offensively. Mainly we were moving the ball up and down through the air. Barry really didn't get moving right away. We knew if we could get him going that would be the icing on the cake. We were clicking as an offensive unit, the defense was stopping them and giving us the ball back. It was a fun game.

The crowd was great, they were so loud. That whole year we won every home game, went undefeated at home. That was the icing on the cake for the fans. They were so loud. When the Dallas offense went on the field you could barely hear anything. I remember seeing the white and silver pom-poms waving. It was really loud and that was definitely a plus for us.

Barry got going and he capped off the game with one of the greatest runs ever. When everybody from Dallas thought he was down, he emerged from the pile. They still show that play in highlights sometimes. He kind of just shook the other team, they thought he was going to go one way, he went the other way for a touchdown [for 47 yards].

As a rookie I thought it was great for me, I thought this would happen all the time. Come to find out years later it's so hard to get into the playoffs and even harder to actually win. That was our last playoff win. We've been to playoffs years afterwards and lost the first game and were run out.

It was something we thought we'd be able to do for years. As a rookie I didn't realize the magnitude of an NFL playoff game.

Other Memorable Moments

The next week's game at Washington was not one for the ages. The Lions lost 41–10.

Still, that playoff win appeared to be the start of good things to come for the Lions. Conover and the Lions made it back to the playoffs in 1993, 1994, and 1995. Loss, loss, bad loss.

Through the 2014 season, that 1991 win over Dallas was the last time the Lions had won in the playoffs.

And the win in Green Bay in the 1991 regular season was the last time the Lions have defeated the Packers in the state of Wisconsin.

The Aftermath

Naturally Conover remains a Lions fan.

"This past year [2014] I've probably been to the most games I've gone to in quite a while," Conover said. "I'm starting to get back involved. The Lions organization is doing a great job of getting former guys back together and making them a part of the organization again. Ryan Hackworth [the Lions community relations manager] is one of the guys. He's doing a great job trying to reach out to the former guys."

Conover does events with other alumni in the community.

"It's so easy with the fan base and the Lions' organization still there giving us support," Conover said. "It works out. They're really stepping out trying to reach out and help us. We've got good support . . . "

When Conover's playing days were over—he only played for the Lions—he moved back to his home state of New Jersey.

Then he made a move maybe not so common with retired NFL players—he went to culinary school. He graduated from the Art Institute of New York, formerly known as the New York Restaurant School.

He developed a passion for cooking when he was young.

"That's something I learned as the oldest of seven," Conover said. "Growing up that was part of my duty to help cook and I enjoyed that. When I was playing I would often cook and some of the guys would come over after practice. I always had a passion for it."

He moved back to the Detroit area in 2007 and worked at the Motor City Casino as a chef before moving to a Kroger's bistro in Northville as the head chef.

These days he's semi-retired which gives him more time in the community and more time to watch the Lions.

He loves coach Jim Caldwell who took over the team in 2014.

"He's an awesome guy. He's got a big heart you can tell he really cares about the players," Conover said. "What you see is what you get from him. He's a motivator, a leader, trying to motivate everyone to play at their best. The players are buying in to what he's telling them, what he's coaching them, and they feel good about him.

"He's first-class all the way, the way he treats you," Conover added. "He's a very humble guy and a passionate coach."

"Hopefully he can build off [2014] and get this team to a Super Bowl, which they definitely deserve. I think it's coming.

"I see them progressing where they're finally getting solid veteran leadership," Conover said. "That was what was important for us in 1991, [and] that's why we were able to be so successful. We had so many veteran leaders. It looks like this team is starting to turn that way. Guys are starting to mature and being there, they're bringing some of the young guys—like I was in 1991 a rookie—bring those guys along. That's what it looks like the team is starting to do—believe in each other, depend on each other, and just lead by example. And it starts with Coach Caldwell."

The 1991 Lions found a formula for success—win all home games, get a home playoff game, and every once in a while give the ball to Barry Sanders.

Now Conover and others hope to see that precious playoff win in 1991 duplicated in coming years.